WALT WHITMAN *&* THE CLASS STRUGGLE

THE IOWA WHITMAN SERIES

Ed Folsom, series editor

ANDREW LAWSON

Walt Whitman

& THE CLASS STRUGGLE

University of Iowa Press IOWA CITY

University of Iowa Press, Iowa City 52242
Copyright © 2006 by the University of Iowa Press
http://www.uiowa.edu/uiowapress
All rights reserved
Printed in the United States of America
Design by Richard Hendel

The University of Iowa Press is a member
of Green Press Initiative and is committed to
preserving natural resources.

Printed on acid-free paper

Library of Congress Cataloging-in-Publication Data
Lawson, Andrew, 1959 Jul.–
Walt Whitman and the class struggle / Andrew Lawson.
p.   cm.—(The Iowa Whitman series)
Includes bibliographical references and index.
ISBN 0-87745-973-8 (cloth)
1. Whitman, Walt, 1819–1892—Political and social views.
2. Literature and society—United States—History—19th
century.   3. Social classes in literature.   4. Social conflict in
literature.   I. Title.   II. Iowa Whitman series.
PS3242.S58.L39 2006   2005053817

06 07 08 09 10 C 5 4 3 2 1

CONTENTS

ACKNOWLEDGMENTS

In its early stages the research for this book was supported by sabbatical leave and a travel grant given by the School of Humanities and Social Sciences at Staffordshire University. My colleagues in English gave generous practical support by taking up additional teaching and administration during my absence. My thanks to Aidan Arrowsmith, Peter Heaney, Laura Peters, and Shaun Richards.

Parts of the book have appeared previously. An earlier version of chapter 1 was published as "'Spending for Vast Returns': Sex, Class, and Commerce in the First *Leaves of Grass,*" *American Literature* 75.2 (June 2003); parts of chapters 2 and 3 appeared in preliminary form as "'Song of Myself' and the Class Struggle in Language," *Textual Practice* 18.3 (Autumn 2004). I'm grateful to the editors and readers of these journals, particularly to Frances Kerr and Peter Nicholls. For their professional skill and patience in the process of turning the manuscript into a book, my grateful thanks to Holly Carver, Charlotte Wright, and Rebecca Marsh. For their advice and encouragement of this and other projects over the years, I want to thank Thomas Augst, Rosemarie K. Bank, Marshall Brown, Burton Hatlen, Brian Jarvis, Ron Loewinsohn, Ian McQuire, and Barrett Watten.

It was Barry Taylor who first piqued my interest in Whitman by sharing with me his delight in what he called, in his typically witty and pertinent way, the "crunchy" texture of the verse. I've been lucky to have many similarly fruitful conversations with him over the years. Susan Brook, Sandra Courtman, and Peter Knight provided me with expert, detailed comments on the chapters as they emerged and helped me not just to clarify my arguments but to understand what I was attempting. I also benefited greatly from the authority and range of Ed Folsom's knowledge of Whitman scholarship. Richard Godden subjected the first chapter to a deeply informed and searching critique, then calmly set the challenge I attempt to meet in the rest of the book. My specific debts to him are recorded in the footnotes, but his example and influence have been crucial and pervasive.

In writing about class I found I was also writing about family, and I've been more than fortunate in my own. My parents supported me unfailingly through an education that must have seemed interminable. My parents-in-law, Anne Thompson and Bryan Thompson, offered me warm encouragement and showed a keen interest in the progress of the book. At the heart of the matter always has been Deborah Thompson, who has kept me going while reminding me of what's really important. As does Michael: he is just awesome.

ABBREVIATIONS

AP
Walt Whitman, *An American Primer:
With Facsimiles of the Original Manuscript.*
Baker
Benjamin A. Baker, *A Glance at New York.*
Brooklyn Printer
Whitman, "Death of the Veteran Brooklyn Printer."
CH
Whitman, *Walt Whitman: The Critical Heritage.*
EPF
Whitman, *The Early Poems and the Fiction.*
GF
Whitman, *The Gathering of the Forces.*
J1
Whitman, *Collected Writings of Walt Whitman, The Journalism,*
vol. 1, 1834–1846.
J2
Whitman, *Collected Writings of Walt Whitman, The Journalism,*
vol. 2, 1846–1848.
Leggett
William Leggett, *A Collection of the Political Writings of William Leggett.*
LG
Whitman, *Walt Whitman's Leaves of Grass: The First (1855) Edition.*
NUPM
Whitman, *Notebooks and Unpublished Prose Manuscripts.*
NYD
Whitman, *New York Dissected: A Sheaf of Recently Discovered Newspaper
Articles by the Author of "Leaves of Grass."*
PW
Whitman, *Prose Works 1892.*

RE

  Whitman, *Leaves of Grass: Reader's Edition.*

TW

  Whitman, "Talbot Wilson" notebook.

UPP

  Whitman, *Uncollected Poetry and Prose of Walt Whitman.*

WWW

  Whitman, *Walt Whitman's Workshop.*

INTRODUCTION: THE WHITMAN MYTH

On July 4, 1855, a curious new volume could be found on Nassau Street, New York, on sale at two dollars. The book was of an unusual, quarto size and bound in dark green pebbled cloth. The title, *Leaves of Grass*, was stamped on the cover in gold letters that, somewhat incongruously, sprouted a profusion of leaves and sent down a dense tangle of roots. Anyone browsing at the Nassau Street bookstore would, on opening the book, have come across an engraving of a bearded man in a "wideawake" hat, his drawstring vest visible beneath his open-necked shirt, his steady, level gaze meeting his or hers with equal parts effrontery, good humor, and challenge: an image that might have been contrived to embody the idea of the authentic American as Adam, "a figure of heroic innocence and vast potentialities, poised at the start of a new history" (fig. 1).[1] The browser would then have discovered ten pages of double-columned, densely printed type, resembling those of a newspaper, with the boosterish tone of a political manifesto ("America does not repel the past or what it has produced under its forms"). Unless finally deterred, the casual reader would then have found twelve untitled, unrhymed poems in irregular stanzas, the first longer than the rest put together and beginning in extravagantly capitalized form:

I CELEBRATE myself,
And what I assume you shall assume,
For every atom belonging to me as good belongs to you. (*LG* 25)

As a physical object, *Leaves of Grass* resonates with contradictions, its hefty price and high-toned cover clashing with its vaguely plebeian frontispiece and journalistic preface. Something in its appearance or contents seems to have alarmed the Nassau Street bookseller, because it was quickly withdrawn from sale. The book was next offered at the phrenological cabinet of Fowlers and Wells in Manhattan and at the firm's establishment on Washington Street, Brooklyn.

The publication of *Leaves of Grass* in 1855 has been called, by Whitman's most recent biographer, the "central literary event of the nineteenth

1. *Frontispiece to Walt Whitman,* Leaves of Grass *(1st edition, Brooklyn, New York: the author, 1855). Courtesy of the Library of Congress, Prints and Photographs Division, LC-USZ62–8274.*

century."[2] But what, if anything, justifies such a claim? It was Malcolm Cowley who first argued for the centrality of this first edition of *Leaves of Grass*. Cowley identified the source of Whitman's originality in his intense individualism: the defiant way in which Whitman takes himself as his subject and offers himself to his readers in all his "gross" and "mystical" particularity, the essential unity of flesh and spirit unabashedly proclaimed (*LG* 43). Foregrounding an ordinary human body and its urges and offering a new kind of avowedly personal, oddly vulnerable speaking voice, *Leaves of Grass* deserves the status of literary event.

But Cowley made another claim, which, I think, rings less convincingly: that, with the 1855 book, Whitman "created the new personality of the proletarian bard" (*LG* viii). The claim is echoed by more recent Whitman scholars, who find a "working-class fervor" in Whitman's unconventional verse, a projection of "proletarian energies and sympathies."[3] The iconic image of the frontispiece might fit this billing, presenting the physical assertiveness and perhaps touchy pride of a man who works with his hands. But a reading of the book's long poem, later titled "Song of Myself," yields little that is particularly "proletarian" in its diction. On the contrary, Whitman flourishes an increasing number of learned and fancy words at the reader: he speaks of the "equanimity" of things (27), sounds music through his "embouchures" (42), directs our attention to "old cartouches" (47), extols his "amies" (46), and salutes his "[e]leves" (69). His famously democratic catalogs include, along with the familiar raftsmen, hunters, and ranchers, a "novice beginning experient of myriads of seasons" (40). Whatever else might be said about it, this is patently not the working-class dialect of antebellum New York. Indeed, anyone who probed a little into the cultural history of Whitman's time and place would be struck by how sharply his poetry diverges from the Irish, German, or black speech then gaining representation on the New York stage in popular plays like Benjamin A. Baker's *A Glance at New York* in 1848, in penny newspapers like the *New York Herald*, and in a whole range of sensational, mass-market literature, "masculine, profane, tangible."[4] At the same time, most readers of "Song of Myself" will occasionally come across examples of the "living and buried" vernacular speech that can be found "vibrating" in the poem (32): the butcher boy's "shuffle and breakdown" (34), the declaration that "life is a suck and a sell" (43), that "[w]ashes and razors" are for "foofoos" (46). At odd moments, the self-consciously "educated" diction slips enough for the poem to register at least some of the slang of Whitman's Manhattan, its "howls restrained by decorum" (32).

Two related problems concerning the first edition of *Leaves of Grass* interest me here. First, the problem of deciding exactly what kind of political identity or persona Whitman presents and whether there is any slippage between persona and identity, between the optative voice of the poetry, with its rather official-sounding declarations about the diversity and largeness of America, and what can be inferred about the man staring out at the reader in his working clothes. Second, the problem of the linguistic texture of *Leaves of Grass*: its somewhat aggressively mixed diction, its pointed, perhaps even charged confrontations between high and low registers. These problems suggest other questions—about how historically specific the poetry is and about how one goes about defining and describing that specificity. We now know a good deal about the historical context of *Leaves of Grass* and about the cultural politics of the antebellum period.[5] But while Whitman has been admirably well located within his time and place, it seems to me that his class identity has been either assumed or ignored or fixed wide of the mark—and that, as a result, a great deal of what Whitman has to say about the institutions of culture and the politics of class has been missed, or else misinterpreted, by even the most "revisionary" of his readers.

To take one example, in his discussion of "Song of Myself," Donald Pease is alert to the "full itinerary" of Whitman's personae, to the plurality of "selves" whose predilections and experiences feed into the composite, speaking "self" of the poem: "teacher, editor, dandy, stroller, ward leader, compositor, delegate, orator, carpenter, politician, house-builder."[6] Pease argues that Whitman's poetry "silently aspired to mediate" between a "literary clientele" and a constituency of "working-class men and women," bringing "representatives of the working-class elbow to elbow with the literary elite."[7] The argument is plausible, not least because it is the avowed intention of Whitman in the 1855 preface to be the "arbiter of the diverse" (*LG* 8). It's an established practice in Whitman scholarship to look for this kind of corroborating evidence in Whitman's voluminous prose writings, matching the intricacies and indirections of the poetry to plainer, more discursive statements.

Manifold inconsistencies and changes of tack can, however, be found within the prose as within the poetry. At the close of the preface, Whitman announces that the "swarms of the polished" and the polite "float off and leave no remembrance" (*LG* 23). The tone switches abruptly here, as the lofty and the idealistic paeans to American diversity give way to overt class abuse: the "arbitrating" voice becomes edgy, rebarbative, mocking. Similarly, in the opening sections of "Song of Myself," Whitman tells us he is quitting the perfumed literary salon for the more bracing atmosphere of the "bank by the wood," where he will become "undisguised and naked" (25). If this is mediation or arbitration between polarized social formations, then it is of a distinctly problematic kind. A momentary cross-class intimacy is abruptly broken up—for reasons which remain troublingly obscure. The declension from "arbiter of the diverse" to "swarms of the polished" needs some accounting for: it indicates that, in order to understand Whitman's class politics, we are going to have to come to grips with his use of different kinds of language.

Scholars who have devoted particular attention to Whitman's language tend to place the same stress on mediation and inclusiveness as those who describe Whitman's "pluralist" political stance. James Perrin Warren elucidates Whitman's "theory of language" from his assorted essays and notebook entries on the subject and from the preface, where Whitman writes of how the English language "befriends the grand American expression": "On the tough stock of a race who through all change of circumstances was never without the idea of political liberty . . . it has attracted the terms of daintier and gayer and subtler and more elegant tongues" (*LG* 22–23). Whitman here follows an "organic" conception of the English language, seeing it as an "ensemble," a hybrid of earthy, Anglo-Saxon words and refined borrowings from French and Latin.[8] Its hospitable absorptiveness shows American English to be the natural expression of the nation's democratic spirit, a harmonious blend of the traditional and the modern, the learned and the colloquial. The case for Whitman as the pioneer of "American Eclectic," a technique based on "pluralistic juxtapositions," is put by Edwin Fussell, who declares that Whitman "simply draws upon whatever vocabularies he likes, mainly the American vernacular, but also archaisms, poeticisms, neologisms, foreign borrowings, new coinages, slang, and toward this psychedelic eclecticism of vocabularies he maintains an attitude of imperturbable tranquility."[9] The figure of the American Adam lurks behind this characterization of Whitman's eclecticism—a figure so "emancipated from history" that he can take what he wants from any particular vocabulary with a "childlike cheerfulness."[10]

In a curious way, Whitman's putative "proletarian" status supports this understanding of his absorptive linguistic practice. Thus, for John P. McWilliams, Whitman can incorporate "slang, colloquialisms, and foreign words into a fully polyglossic American idiom . . . precisely because it was 'barbaric yawp.'" Whitman's proletarian innocence enables him to break the rules of Augustan decorum and infuse poetry with a new and "bras[h]" vitality.[11] "Brash" here means something like "spontaneous, unaffected, uneducated." Like "proletarian" in Cowley's usage, the word refers vaguely to the lower orders of society, while carefully sealing that particular space off from any history of political conflicts. "Brash" betokens innocence and perpetuates the myth of Whitman as brawny American Adam. But, in fact, a whole range of class tensions lie just beneath the surface of Whitman's language—tensions that, once examined, should lead us toward a reconsideration of both his political identity and his distinctive use of language.

Whitman was not actually a member of the "working class" but an artisan possessed of a skilled trade and a measure of independence. Leaving school at the age of twelve, he began as an apprentice printer, became a newspaper editor, failed in this, and turned to his father's trade of carpentry and house building before writing *Leaves of Grass*. Whitman did not labor in the factories and sweatshops of Manhattan, and in his career as a journalist he gained increasingly in "respectability" and reputation. It is more accurate, I think, to see Whitman as belonging to the antebellum lower middle class: a class location that is more complex and indeterminate than that of the "proletarian" and one that needs to be understood in its historical particularity.

In the aftermath of the 1837 Panic, Whitman joined the breakaway Equal Rights faction of the Democratic Party known as the Locofocos (named after the brand of friction matches its members used when the lights were turned out on them at a Tammany Hall meeting). Representing the interests not of the working class but of small producers, the Locofocos broke with the Democrats over the older party's support for monopoly. A particular source of resentment was the granting of special charters to corporations by state legislatures and the reluctance of banks to provide credit to new men in business.[12] The Columbia student George Templeton Strong, who was to become a prominent Whig lawyer, disdainfully records a "Locofoco meeting in the Park" in April 1837, which "looked like a convention of loafers from all quarters of the world."[13] In the presidential election year of 1840, Whitman wrote an article for the *Long-Island Democrat* ironically proposing "getting up a regular ticket" for a political party of "loafers" to oppose the "manufacturing privileges" of the Whigs—where "loafer" is a synonym for "Locofoco Democrat" (*J1* 28). The struggle between classes in this period was thus also a struggle over the political meanings of the vernacular. The opening line of "Song of Myself," "I loafe and invite my soul," retains something of this charge of class invective.

But the line also carries a sign of Whitman's lower-middle-class bid for cultural distinction by juxtaposing its vernacular verb with the high-flown, Emersonian language of the soul. Whitman was exposed to this language when he heard Emerson's lecture "The Poet" at the New York Society on March 5, 1842. "The transcendentalists had a very full house on Saturday evening," Whitman told the readers of the *New York Aurora*, going on to notice the presence in the audience of "beautiful maids" and "bluestockings," as well as "several interesting men with Byron collars; lawyers, doctors, and parsons; Grahamites and abolitionists; sage editors, a few of whom were taking notes; and all the other species of literati" (*J1* 44). As James Russell Lowell recalled, Emerson appealed to a "promiscuous crowd," drawn from across the range of the antebellum middle class.[14] In Donald M. Scott's useful description, these were "aspiring and ambitious" people who "perceived themselves in motion, in a state of preparation or expectation," people with "a desire for useful knowledge that would give them the hold on life that their aspirations seemed to require."[15] On this particular March day, Emerson told his listeners that "[e]xpression" was "prosperity," that they were all poets in the sense that they each "burn[ed]" with the need for expression, verbal and physical, and that it is "a wondrous power to report the inner man adequately to multitudes of men, and bring one's character to bear on others."[16] This is just the kind of message calculated to appeal to those middle-class aspirants whose only capital is their character. It is easy to imagine the faces of Emerson's audience "agleam with pale intellectual light, eager with pleased attention"—Whitman's face, perhaps, especially agleam, especially eager.[17]

Ralph Waldo Emerson made his living on the public-lecture circuit based in town lyceums and young men's associations. In a notebook entry for 1839, he hymns the lyceum's social diversity: "All the breadth & versatility of the most liberal conversation the most high the most low the most personal the most local topics, all are permitted, and all may be combined in one speech; it is a panharmonicon,—every note on the lowest gamut, from the explosion of cannon, to the tinkle of a guitar."[18] Like Whitman's critics, Emerson reads the lyceum as an enriching assemblage of languages where social differences and pressures—the high and the low, the explosion of cannon—are defused and disarmed by the simple act of recognition.

But Whitman is less inclined toward celebration. Where Emerson hears universal harmony in the lyceum, Whitman is reminded of class division. In an unpublished essay on language, "The Primer of Words," Whitman declares that he wants a "renovated English speech in America," a speech distinct from "the etiquette of saloons," from occasions that are "for a coterie, a bon soir or two" (*AP* 2). In "Song of Myself," Whitman draws attention to his status as a man whose stock of cultural capital is relatively low:

> My signs are a rain-proof coat and good shoes and a staff cut from the
>   woods;
> No friend of mine takes his ease in my chair,
> I have no chair, nor church nor philosophy;
> I lead no man to a dinner-table or library or exchange [. . .]. (*LG* 80)

This is a catalog not of democratic diversity but of social and cultural disadvantage. The literary culture offered by the lyceum is an ambivalent commodity for the lower-middle-class autodidact, since it awakens a sense of social injustice and class privilege even as it urges the self on to achievement and distinction.

A tendency among critics has been to simply celebrate the "heteroglossia" of Whitman's text and the "carnivalesque" atmosphere of the antebellum period—deploying Mikhail Bakhtin's by now well-worn terms.

"[D]emocratic America," David Reynolds claims, "was a kind of carnival culture, one that abolished the social distance between people and yoked together the high and the low in an atmosphere of jolly relativity."[19] For Reynolds, *Leaves of Grass* issues a "proclamation" of "fertile cultural interactions, made in language that dissolve[s] the boundaries between prose and poetry, between polite diction and slang."[20] "Carnival" becomes a synonym for "cultural pluralism," with Bakhtin and Whitman conscripted into the service of what Gary Saul Morson calls "American progressive ideals."[21] But, as Ken Hirschkop observes, "[s]ocial critique does not flow from the mere recognition that there are lots of us about."[22] Whitman's poetry shows language to be heterogeneous but also stratified, marked by a hierarchy of value. Elite and popular accents clash against each other in the antebellum period; this struggle, however, is conducted not in an "atmosphere of jolly relativity" but within a context of economic inequality and political conflict.

The Whitman whose voice finds poetic expression in the first *Leaves of Grass* seems to me to be rather less aloof and idealistic than has been supposed, less the equable mediator than the class-conscious provocateur. Another way of putting this would be to say that Whitman, in the journalism as in the poetry, is *both* a democratic yea-sayer *and* a sometimes embittered, always pointed critic of elite pretension.[23] Whitman the radical artisan opposed monopoly and privilege because, like other small producers, he wanted to see the way cleared for opportunity and enterprise. Far from adopting an oppositional, "proletarian" position toward the market revolution of the Jacksonian period, Whitman embraced the market for the scope it offered to the self-made man. In the first chapter of this book, I read *Leaves of Grass* as the ambivalent working-through of the emotional and psychological costs of this embrace and describe what the poetry reveals of the stresses of self-making.

Whitman's lower-middle-class location shaped his relation to language and culture. As an artisan and autodidact, Whitman craved the signs and tokens of cultural distinction possessed more securely by the educated upper middle class he opposed politically.[24] In this contradiction, I argue across the remaining chapters, lies the solution to the problem of Whitman's mixed diction, its continual oscillation between the refined and the coarse, its inability to settle into any consistent class accent, any unified voice. Whitman's essential dilemma was that he had a place neither in the refined upper middle class nor in the rowdy working-class cultures of antebellum New York. The mixed diction of "Song of Myself" reflects this shifting, ambiguous space between classes, as Whitman searches for a "virtuous middle ground" but is condemned to wander between sharply opposed languages—seeking to mediate at one moment, drawn into conflict the next.[25]

By "class struggle" I therefore mean two things. First, I mean the diverse ways in which individuals like Whitman express their opposition to the structured inequalities that prevail in the antebellum period—opposition that could involve the organizing of strikes against employers, the writing of newspaper articles protesting wealth and privilege, antislavery agitation against "the lords of the lash and the loom," or the pelting of English actors on the stage. But I also mean the phrase to suggest the struggle a lower-middle-class individual like Whitman has with his own class identity, with its tensions and contradictions. Admittedly, I end up with an altogether darker, more conflicted Whitman than the one we have been used to dealing with, one inclined to bardic celebration but also to withering denunciation and sly, sarcastic jabs. An insistent impulse toward satire and mockery, it seems to me, lies behind Whitman's bardic celebration of America, a tone of bitterness and insecurity that keeps breaking through the bonhomie and braggadocio. But there is something to learn from Whitman's tone about life in the market for the lower middle class, and the first *Leaves of Grass* provides lessons in how a writer uses the resources of language to craft a necessarily ambivalent response to the contradictions of life in a class society.

By insisting on overturning myths, I don't pretend to be able to conjure the "real, flesh-and-blood" Whitman. But I do claim that there is a "historically identifiable person" behind *Leaves of Grass*, one whose identity can be reconstructed from the multitudinous written traces that person has deposited in the archive—without, as Gramsci says, leaving an inventory.[26] *Leaves of Grass* is a densely historical text in which "[e]ach word tastes of the context and contexts in which it has lived its socially charged life."[27] I therefore spend some time describing Whitman's engagement with a variety of antebellum literary genres, including transcendentalism, southwestern humor, political journalism, urban sensationalism, philology, sexology, and astronomy. To read *Leaves of Grass* with any degree of precision and purpose, we need to be able to catch at least some of its historical flavor: to grasp the ways in which its multifaceted language reflects the bewilderingly rich and complex range of texts circulating within the print culture of the antebellum period.

During the 1830s and 1840s, an ocean of print flooded the American market. Aided by the invention of the rapid cylinder press and by the absence of international copyright agreements, publishing firms issued pirated editions of popular novels by authors like Charles Dickens and Eugene Sue, along with cheap reprints of everything from evangelical tracts and works of popular science to agricultural, medical, legal, and literary texts, in "a dissemination of reading" that appeared to offer "egalitarian access to the benefits of elite culture."[28] As the editor of the *Brooklyn Eagle*, Whitman received a regular supply of review copies from publishers, finding himself "surrounded by the current literature of [his] age," supported by such a quantity of "thought and facts evolved from master-minds" that he felt he could not possibly "*lag behind*" (*J2* 112; emphasis in original). Whitman could feast at "a literary banquet" in which "treasures of mind, far more valuable than any physical treasures," were "made accessible to the poor and simple, alike with rich and learned" (201). Whitman pointed out to his readers that for twelve and a half cents a single number of Littell's *Living Age* would furnish "the Life and Correspondence of David Hume, from the Quarterly—Historical Pictures of the Middle Ages, from the Athenæum—a Coming Change in Europe, from the Times—Life and Adventures of Miss Robinson Crusoe, from Punch—and a long string of capital things, also, selected with taste, and printed in clear good style" (25). Through a program of "useful" reading, the lower-middle-class autodidact could draw on this kind of miscellany, obtaining needed information on etiquette, on dress and deportment, and on the topics of civilized discourse. Literary recreation developed a capacity for "active critical judgment" and self-reflection, building the kind of character necessary for success in a competitive, commercial society, while supplying the refinements of the bourgeois parlor.[29] Whether enthusing over *Self-Culture* by William Ellery Channing or welcoming the Harper brothers' *Memoirs of the Most Eminent*

American Mechanics, Whitman's *Eagle* notices advance the cause of "unlimited self-improvement," defining the cultivation of "the powers of the mind" as "the first duty of a good citizen" (*J2* 106).

The Whitman who went on to write "Song of Myself" was the product of a course of wide, undirected, necessarily haphazard reading. There is the sense of a vital idea falling into place when Whitman reads Park Godwin's translation of *The Autobiography of Goethe* (1846) and notices that the work "seems shaped with the intention of rendering a history of soul and body's growth," a history written "as an intelligent man would to a refined and sincere friend" (*J2* 126, 289). But the impetus toward accounting for personal growth was felt by many lower-middle-class souls, who found that they were able, as Channing put it, "to discern not only what we already are, but what we may become, to see in ourselves germs and promises of a growth to which no bounds can be set, to dart beyond what we have actually gained to the idea of Perfection as the end of our being."[30]

But contradictions and frictions exist beneath the "seeming boundlessness" of antebellum print culture.[31] As Michel de Certeau points out, the borders of literary culture are policed by "socially authorized professionals and intellectuals," whose job is to define the correct canons of taste, to construct an approved list of authors, and to fix the meanings of the text for its readers.[32] In this sense, the literary text is "a cultural weapon, a private hunting reserve."[33] But the reader always "invents in texts something different" from the prescribed, official meaning: he or she "combines their fragments and creates something unknown in the space organized by [the texts'] capacity for allowing an indefinite plurality of meanings."[34] Autodidact readers, in particular, are "travelers": they "move across lands belonging to someone else, like nomads poaching their way across fields they did not write."[35] A reader of Littell's *Living Age*, with its miscellany of unauthorized reprints from British literary periodicals, may aspire to "a cosmopolitan worldliness and detachment," but he or she is literally "poaching on the commons" of an elite literary culture.[36] Whitman, in the preface to *Leaves of Grass*, asserts that this culture is legitimately owned by those able to make the best use of it. The true "owner of the library" is "not he who holds a legal title to it having bought and paid for it." Instead, Whitman argues, "[a]ny one and every one is owner of the library" who can read "all the varieties of tongues and subjects and styles," making something "supple and powerful and rich and large" out of them (*LG* 17).

The poacher is faced with the choice of consuming the literary goods according to the owner's taste or constructing an alternative system of cultural value for him- or herself. As he perused the latest volumes in Putnam's "Library of Choice Reading" or the reprints of classic English authors issued by the Harper brothers, Whitman began to fashion both a discriminating, eclectic taste and a set of resentments against cultural authorities of different kinds. In his book reviews, Whitman is highly appreciative of the aesthetic appeal of books, confessing to the *Eagle*'s readers "a fondness for a tastily illustrated work" (*J2* 11). In literary works, Whitman values "an elegant ease of style" (53), the "[e]llegant simplicity" (138) of "the maturer polished taste" (145). For Whitman, "quiet polish" (159) bespeaks "legitimate refinement" (138). This quiet good taste is legitimate because it is not that of the flashy nouveau riches: "we are absolutely sick to nausea of the patent-leather, curled hair, 'japonicadom' style," Whitman exclaims (138). But quiet good taste also reflects the proud autonomy of the self-cultured, lower-middle-class man, who has made his way without the benefit of a classical education or those "[m]othy antiquated reasoners who merely think and act through the minds and eyes of the Past" (148). When Whitman promises the reader of "Song of Myself" that he or she will "no longer take things at second or third hand," nor "look through the eyes of the dead," nor "feed on the spectres in books" (*LG* 26), he is asserting both this kind of autonomy and the autodidact's troubled sense of having gained his knowledge through precisely such a set of complex mediations.

Whitman "scavenged, paraphrased, and pastiched" in the shadows cast by literary authority.[37] In this, he resembles the largely self-educated clerks of the antebellum metropolis, whose life world is described by Thomas Augst. These men were "acutely aware of the moral authority and social prestige that the classical curriculum conferred on members of the traditional professions in the ministry, education, and the law"—and just as aware of their lack of such credentials.[38] "Making their haphazard way to uncertain futures," they "swam in a field of cultural debris, among remnants of ethical systems from which they fashioned a complex, fragmented sense of identity."[39] *Leaves of Grass* manifests the creative haphazardness, the eclectic taste, and the capacity for syncretic combinations of information from diverse fields of knowledge that characterize this lower-middle-class reading formation. It is a book composed out of what Whitman called "[s]craps of [e]ducation," those "[f]ragments" that, when "united," make up "the intellectual storehouse" (*J2* 165).[40] But Whitman's poetry is also marked by a gnawing class consciousness: a sense of exclusion from literary culture, combined with an equally strong sense of entitlement to it.

The challenge of reading Whitman historically, it seems to me, is first of all to accurately describe his class location; then to identify the class accents that inflect almost every word of the poetry; and, finally, to trace those accents back to the social and political conditions that determined them—to the class struggles and social tensions of antebellum New York. For at stake in Whitman's heteroglot style is the issue of cultural authority: the social power implied by the possession of literary language and the challenge to that power mounted by other less legitimate languages: the abrasive class accents of jargon, cant, and slang. As Whitman phrases the issue in *An American Primer*, "[n]ames are the turning point of who shall be master" (34).

Whitman's lower-middle-class location placed him in a determinate relation to literary language and to the authority claimed and conferred by that language. The relation is that of the provincial outsider who steps across the metropolitan threshold—uncertain of his ground but determined to make his mark. What he finds in the stock of cultural capital he uses for his own purposes, but he is always in a fundamentally estranged relation to it. In reading the first *Leaves of Grass*, my aim is to keep alive a sense of its profound oddity and obliqueness and to describe the conflicted social space Whitman writes from, the kind of space that produces a drive toward naturalness that is also a bid for distinction: leaves of grass in letters of gold.

WALT WHITMAN *&* THE CLASS STRUGGLE

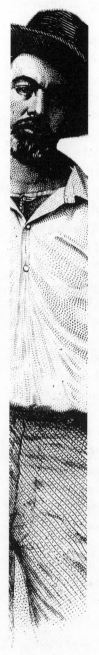

1 : SEX, CLASS, & COMMERCE

Whitman hoped to orchestrate the entry of *Leaves of Grass* into literary history through a series of self-publicizing acts. For the first edition of 1855, he placed the portrait of himself by Samuel Hollyer opposite the title page. The portrait shows Whitman with "hat on, shirt open, head cocked, arm akimbo," positively reeking of streetwise physicality in his "first poetic pose," that of the "worker/poet" (fig. 1).[1] Then, some five hundred lines into the poem, a name is abruptly attached to what has been an anonymous "I": "Walt Whitman, an American, one of the roughs, a kosmos" (*LG* 48). Finally, there is the series of three anonymous reviews Whitman published of his own work, beginning in the *United States Review*, in which he elaborates on his own self-representation: "[o]ne of the roughs, large, proud, affectionate, eating, drinking, and breeding, his costume manly and free[,] . . . self-reliant, with haughty eyes, assuming to himself all the attributes of his country, steps Walt Whitman into literature" (*CH* 34, 35). This self-portrait informs the canonical Whitman, created by F. O. Matthiessen in *American Renaissance* (1941). "As the son of a common man, as a casual worker in his own turn," Matthiessen tells us, Whitman "knew how the poor really lived"; in his political and economic views he is "typical of the aspirations and struggles of the working class in the America of his time."[2]

But Whitman's identity with "working class" life is not as straightforward as it might seem, even in his own self-representations. In another unsigned review, for the *Brooklyn Daily Times*, Whitman describes himself as "a man who is art-and-part of the commonalty," a man who so "loves the streets" that he would "leave a select soiree of elegant people any time to go with tumultuous men, roughs, receive their caresses and welcome, listen to their noise, oaths, smut, fluency, laughter, repartee" (*CH* 43). Here, Whitman delineates the polarized social spaces of antebellum New York: a domestic, feminized space composed of "elegant people" and a homosocial, working-class world of "tumultuous men."[3] But his own position is somewhere ambiguously in between, a liminal space marked by "leaving" one in order to "go with" the other. The Whitman presented here seems to have a foot in both camps. The potentially awkward and unsettling effects of this ambiguous identity are brought out in Stephen Alonzo Schoff's engraving, used as the frontispiece in Whitman's first major revision of *Leaves of Grass* (1860; fig. 2). Gone is the "rough's" open-necked physicality of 1855. In its place is a much more conventional, head-and-shoulders portrait of a bearded but immaculately coiffured man, wearing a Windsor tie and jacket—the image of a man who appears ready to join a select soiree.

In these self-reviews and revisions, Whitman puts his self-image into circulation as a figure of liminality, constructing an identity that crosses class boundaries with apparent ease. This fluid self, I will be arguing, is a feature of a market society characterized by the notion of exchange.[4] And this marketing of the self is particularly pronounced among a lower middle class whose identities are dependent on both their limited resources and their own resourcefulness. As a journeyman printer who worked variously as a teacher, carpenter, journalist, and government clerk, Whitman belonged to a Jacksonian lower middle class undergoing the transition from an agrarian, artisanal culture to an urban, market economy. The artisan system's hierarchical order of owner-master, skilled journeyman, and apprentice held out the reasonable expectation that apprentices would eventually become masters, achieving not wealth necessarily but at the very least a competency. In medieval guild fashion, buying and selling were carefully regulated according to a list of "just" prices. The essence of the artisan system was small property, craft skill, and self-contracting labor. Artisans were part of the antebellum "lower" middle class because, like shopkeepers and small farmers, they had a measure of independence lacking among the unskilled working class. But their position in society was below that of the larger property holders of the solidly middle class: merchants, professionals, and the new group of factory owners.[5]

2. *Frontispiece to Walt Whitman,* Leaves of Grass *(3rd edition, Boston: Thayer and Eldridge, 1860). Courtesy of the Library of Congress, Prints and Photographs Division, LC-USZ62–82796.*

What radically unsettles the position of artisans in the Jacksonian period is the rise of the market economy, which substitutes market value for just price and dismantles the hierarchy of the artisan system by replacing apprenticeship with waged labor. The free market's levelling of hierarchy was potentially liberating: it offered the prospect of a new kind of individual mobility and the opportunity to accumulate wealth through market speculation and expansion. But it also introduced a new set of contingencies: the known and familiar rituals of the trades were dissolved by the contractual relations of the market, while journeymen found their living standards driven down and their skills devalued.[6] Whitman's first poetic production is marked by a mixture of self-assertion and anxiety, which can be traced to the uncertain position of the lower middle class as it moves from agrarian folkways to the urban marketplace. Whitman's affirmative statements about the market are made directly in *Leaves of Grass* and its preface; but the doubts and anxieties are expressed, in a kind of reverse sublimation, through the poetry's unsettling eroticism, its foregrounding of the destabilizing effects of desire. In order to read *Leaves of Grass* for what it has to say about the market, I want first of all to locate Whitman's position within the Jacksonian lower middle class via an examination of its most spectacular representative, the Bowery b'hoy.

Whitman's first performance as worker/poet produced the desired response from contemporary reviewers, who almost immediately identified him with the street culture of antebellum New York. Reviewing the first *Leaves of Grass*, the *New York Daily News* put together the "crush hat and red shirt open at the neck, without waistcoat or jacket," with the poet's stance, "one hand on his hip and the other thrust into his pocket," to come up with "Walt Whitman, the b'hoy poet," who, writing "on his muscle," produces lines of "extraordinary vigor."[7] The *Washington Daily National Intelligencer* declared that "[i]f the artist has faithfully depicted his effigy, Walt is indeed 'one of the roughs,' for his picture would answer equally well for a 'Bowery boy.'"[8] A journeyman or apprentice in one of the traditional trades, the Bowery b'hoy emerged from the volunteer fire companies of the 1830s with a new addiction to style and dash that made him a stock figure in the journalism and literary expression of the antebellum period and the hero of Benjamin A. Baker's wildly popular play *A Glance at New York* in 1848. Strolling the Bowery in his costume of stovepipe hat, red flannel shirt, check trousers, and heavy boots "designed for use in slaughterhouses and at fires," the b'hoy became the incarnation of republican virtue in an urban setting—fiercely independent, self-reliant, and free; he was the "joyous, riotous, rollicking, good-natured b'hoy strutting home from the field of his bloodless prowess."[9] Whitman deliberately cultivated an identification with the metropolitan type of the Bowery b'hoy, providing both his contemporaries and later critics with a literary persona through which to read him.[10]

But who exactly were the b'hoys, and what accounts for the lavish attention paid to them by antebellum writers? Charles Haswell, in his *Reminiscences of an Octogenarian of the City of New York* (1896), is emphatic that the b'hoy was "not an idler and a corner lounger, but mostly an apprentice, generally to a butcher."[11] Butchering is described by Sean Wilentz as one of the "strongholds of the artisan system," where a master, once installed, "stood a good chance of prospering" in a still-regulated market able to resist the effects of proletarianization.[12] Butchers thus remained aloof from the trade-union militancy of the workingmen's movement, the "radical journeymen's protest" that had, by the 1840s, failed to resist the downward pressure on wages.[13] In addition, the butchers' daily routines of "intense labor followed by leisurely afternoons and evenings" allowed them greater opportunities than other craftsmen had for recreation and "public show."[14]

The Bowery b'hoy thus "drew his identity from an awareness of a set of cultural images" rather than the collective class consciousness of organized labor.[15] The first words of Mose in *A Glance at New York* are "I've made up my mind not to run wid der [fire] machine any more," as he begins the problematic process of detaching himself from the "traditionalist" working-class culture represented by the fire company and fashioning himself as an individual actor in a market society (Baker 171).[16] For the rest of the play, Mose is pulled between Bowery and Broadway, rudeness and respectability, through his acquaintance with the business-class Harry Gordon and his greenhorn friend, George Parsells. Mose becomes a liminal figure, involved in a repeated crossing of boundaries. Agreeing to accompany Harry and George to a "ladies' bowling saloon" dressed as women, he is unable to resist kissing the genteel Mrs. Morton (172). Mose then denounces the lower-class denizens of the Loafer's Paradise, a "dirty bar room," as "lazy," explaining that "[t]here's plenty of work in this village for everybody, if they've only a mind to look for it," before breaking the place up with a fight (180). Mose has more irrepressible vitality than the genteel Mortons; but his work ethic is commendable, and his boisterousness is balanced by the vital ingredient of sentiment. Recalling the time he saved a baby from a fire, Mose puts his hand on his heart and declares, "The fire-b'hoys may be a little rough outside, but they're all right here" (183). This message is repeated at the end of the play at the genteel Vauxhall Gardens, where Harry introduces Mose to Mr. Morton, explaining that "[i]n spite of his *outré* manners, he has a noble heart" (196).

George Foster, in *New York by Gas-Light*, also attempts to assimilate Mose into the "great middle class of free life under a republic."[17] In the earlier *New York in Slices*, Foster expands on this point, arguing that the b'hoy's "vulgar rowdyism" is only a distorted expression of his "restrained social instinct, his ambition, his desire to struggle and shine."[18] If the "moral atmosphere" of the city were "purified," the b'hoy would become "a cheerful, industrious, well-to-do, and valuable member of the community," fit to "conquer a piece of the wilderness instead of the Mexicans."[19] But Baker's play ends on a disruptive note, with Mose apologizing to the audience for leaving to help his friend Sykesy out in a fight: "I'm bound to see him righted, 'cos he runs wid our machine, you know" (Baker 196). The ending is offered as an ironic coup de théâtre, but it testifies to the difficulty of any straightforward cooptation of Mose by the middle classes. Running with the machine and dining at Vauxhall Gardens, working at his trade and brawling in a dirty bar, Mose hasn't quite escaped the pull of a traditionalist working-class culture, nor has he gained a secure place in the middle class, despite establishing solid credentials.

A Glance is not so much about "taming" the Bowery b'hoy as an attempt to dramatize the boundaries of a diffuse, lower-middle-class world. The Bowery b'hoy's liminality, his phantasmic, shape-shifting form—loafer-dandy, butcher-boy, member of the great American middle class—is a product of the blurred boundaries of the lower middle class and of an uncertainty about whom these boundaries might include and exclude. For writers like Foster, the b'hoy acts as a symbolic marker of what M. Wynn

Thomas describes as a "hopefully imagined, and desperately idealized, middle way between the two antirepublican extremes of new aristocratic wealth and new slum poverty."[20] But this imaginatively constructed space is never really secure, never able to escape the instability and anxiety it attempts to banish.

The artisanal culture of the antebellum period is thus divided and contradictory. Artisans were skilled workers, many of whom hoped to become small capitalists. Caught in one of the key dilemmas of the Jacksonian period, artisan culture looked back to what E. P. Thompson calls the "moral economy" of "labor republicanism," with its group solidarity and ritual, while at the same time looking forward to the life of the liberal individual in an expanded market. Artisan culture, as Wilentz describes it, is an unstable mixture of radical protest and entrepreneurial energy, of traditional bonds and individual self-assertion. Whitman's clashing portraits, depicting him in succession as rude worker and would-be élégant, offer a dramatic representation of the contradictions inherent in the radically unstable image of the Bowery b'hoy.[21]

Whitman responds to the b'hoy as an exemplary, middle-class individualist: "The boy I love," he writes in "Song of Myself," "becomes a man not through derived power but in his own right" (*LG* 81). "The young mechanic is closest to me," he adds, following this with the affirmation that "there is no trade or employment but the young man following it may become a hero" (82, 83). The fact that the b'hoy emerges in the antebellum period as an individual above all else is, I think, an important clue to the kind of class identity he represents, an identity that is more ambiguous than might be apparent in accounts that celebrate his "boisterous working class consciousness."[22] In *A Pen-and-Ink Panorama of New York City* (1853), Cornelius Mathews observes that the b'hoy was most often "a respectable young butcher" but that he was "sometimes a stout clerk in a jobbing house" and "oftener a junior partner in a wholesale grocery."[23] The artisan-class location of the b'hoy thus overlaps with an emerging white-collar sector in the antebellum city, produced by the growth of manufacturing in competitive markets—a sector comprising "brokers, commission merchants, agents, auctioneers, jobbers, credit reporting agents, advertisers, insurance agents, and freight haulers," the typically atomized individuals of a commercial society.[24]

The Bowery b'hoy belonged to the most mobile and ambitious members of the workforce. Situated precariously at the margins of middle-class respectability, he was a member of the diffuse but distinctive lower middle class of the antebellum period. This "syncretic lower middle class" was composed of both small, independent producers (farmers, artisans, shopkeepers) and the dependent clerks and technicians produced by an emergent industrial capitalist economy.[25] These are the "eager and apprehensive men of small property" identified by Tocqueville as typical Americans—precariously poised between comfort and deprivation in a wildly fluctuating economy.[26] Their vulnerability is voiced by Puffy the baker in Dion Boucicault's popular melodrama set in the aftermath of the 1837 Panic, *The Poor of New York* (1857): "Down in the world now, sir—over speculated like the rest on 'em. I expanded on a new-fangled oven, that was to bake enough bread in six hours to supply the whole United States—got done brown in it myself—subsided into Bowery—expanded again on woffles, caught a second time—obliged to contract into a twelve foot front on Division street. Mrs P. tends the indoor trade—I do a locomotive business in potatoes, and we let our second floor."[27] The Jacksonian America that shaped Whitman's poetic expression is profoundly marked by this mixture of buoyant self-assertion and anxious exposure to the contingencies of the marketplace.

The members of the lower middle class are what Victor Turner terms "threshold people," those liminal persons who "elude or slip through the network of classifications that normally locate states and positions in cultural space."[28] The lower middle class is thus by definition a "complex and unstable" grouping, "polymorphous and tangled." What unity it has derives from a "sense of honorable status," marking its members out from what they regard as the unskilled, less respectable, and wholly dependent working classes.[29] The figure of the Bowery b'hoy identified with by Whitman is bound up with the vicissitudes of this anxious, ambitious class and its struggle to create and defend a symbolic space for itself in the contested spaces of the modern city.

A sense of what motivated Whitman's identification with the Bowery b'hoy can be found in his family history, a story of downward mobility among the "old" lower middle class.[30] His father's family were Long Island landowners and farmers of English origin; his mother's family, the Van Velsors, also owned large holdings on the island. He spent his youth among the "independent farmers, the shopkeepers, and the humbler professional men" of Suffolk County and Brooklyn.[31] Whitman's father, Walter, was apprenticed as a carpenter and built a two-story house on a sixty-acre plot he later purchased. In 1823, Walter took his family to Brooklyn to seek his fortune as a house builder, but his business failed to prosper. Whitman was forced to leave school at the age of eleven to seek employment—first as a clerk, then as an apprentice printer in a trade undergoing its own transition from the artisan system to mass production in the emerging market economy.

As he struggled to make his way as a journalist, Whitman lived a life on the margins, moving from one boardinghouse to another, a member of what Mathews terms "the smaller class of reporters and scribblers" who haunted the Bowery, along with "broken merchants, men in bad hats, [and] gentlemen under indictment at the Sessions."[32] Like Richard Arden, the hero of his unfinished story "The Madman" (1843), Whitman belonged to "a certain class, mostly composed of young men, who occupy a kind of medium between gentility and poverty" (*EPF* 241). It's easy to see how the "prowess, independence, and bravado" of the Bowery b'hoy might appeal to lower-middle-class migrants from the rural hinterland faced with the risks and contingencies of life in the antebellum city.[33]

Whitman's temperance novel, *Franklin Evans; or the Inebriate* (1842), foregrounds these themes of risk and contingency by announcing itself as "the account of a young man, thrown by circumstances amid the vortex of dissipation" (*EPF* 126). The story of a "country youth" who comes to the "great emporium" of New York "to seek his fortune," the novel consists of a series of catastrophic reversals, in which the economic and the psychological mirror each other. Evans is psychologically unstable, "tossed about by every breeze of chance or impulse," and this instability is matched by the market conditions he finds himself thrown into. What mediates psychology and economy, translating inner and outer worlds, is a practice of imitation or speculative identification with a temperate father figure and an intemperate son.

The temperate father is Stephen Lee, the gentleman antiquary Evans meets on the market wagon he takes to the city. The intemperate son is John Colby, "a book-keeper in a mercantile establishment," who initiates Evans into the world of theaters and barrooms. Evans receives an early lesson in the perils of identification: what appears to be a "fashionable gentleman" in a box at the theater turns out to be a waiter at an oyster-house; the charming "hoyden" who takes his fancy on the stage is revealed to be a "coarse" and "blear-eyed" slattern consuming pies in a filthy alley after the show (*EPF* 157, 158). The two poles of business rectitude and pleasurable excess represented by Lee and Colby come into conflict when Evans is entrusted with a vital message from Lee. "Forgetful of my own duty—of my master's honor," says Evans, he spends the evening getting drunk with Colby and is fired (167).

Temporarily reformed, Evans marries Mary, his landlady's daughter, and works in a factory until he is offered the purchase of a vacant lot "in a rather pleasant part of the city." Immediately, "visions of independence and a home of [his] own, and the station of a man of property" float before his eyes. These "dreams of happiness and a competency" are "crushed to the dust" when Evans is forced by his creditors to sell at a loss, whereupon he resumes drinking while Mary dies of shame (*EPF* 174). Intemperance, the sign of a fluctuating moral economy, stands in direct relation of homology to the hazards of the market economy: "sinking, grade by grade" describes both Evans's dissipation and his financial fortunes (175). Alcohol becomes a metonym for money, both predicated on an essential instability, with pleasure and independence revealed as equally illusory.[34]

Franklin Evans describes the lower-middle-class dilemma of the "anxious but ambitious heart." The goal of the "struggle for the envied things of existence" is independence and property, which together secure the boundaries of the self (*EPF* 148). But that struggle is also one that threatens to dissolve the self in daydreams and misrecognitions, in letters gone astray and property lost; the chances are that one will make the wrong investment, marry the wrong person, go "[q]uite mad with resentment and agitation" (185). Ambition, "the poison that rankles in the hearts of men," is the bane of Evans's life as well as its driving force (174). Both the ambition to absorb and accrue experience and the anxiety about the fragile borders of the self exposed by such an ambition are characteristic of a lower-middle-class experience Whitman presents more affirmatively elsewhere in his prose writings.

Although he told Moncure Conway in 1855 that he "chose" to be one of "the laboring class," Whitman meant something historically specific by this designation, at the same time performing his role of worker-poet for the benefit of a visiting Harvard clergyman and associate of Emerson (*CH* 29). In his days as a radical Jacksonian Democrat, Whitman located republican virtue in small producers. In his unpublished political pamphlet "The Eighteenth Presidency!" (1856), Whitman addresses not a class but individual "Workmen" and "Workwomen," to whom the "broad fat states of the West" rightly "belong" (*WWW* 102–3). As M. Wynn Thomas observes, these people are the "independent artisans, mechanics, and sturdy yeoman" of Whitman's "anachronistic imagination," rather than the "numberless members of the wage-earning underclass" who were filling the cities.[35] Later, in *Democratic Vistas* (1871), Whitman committed himself to the "paradox" that "democracy looks with suspicious, ill-satisfied eye upon the very poor, the ignorant, and on those out of business. She asks for men and women with occupations, well-off, owners of houses and acres, and with cash in the bank" (*PW* 2:384). The tensions in Whitman's politics stem from his determination to hold on to an essentially agrarian, lower-middle-class outlook in an urban industrial context—a contradiction that is revealed in his future hopes for an America committed to the production of "comfortable city homesteads and moderate-sized farms, healthy and independent, single separate ownership, fee simple, life in them complete but cheap, within reach of all" (*PW* 2:539). Blurred class boundaries now serve to obscure the unpalatable urban realities of the Gilded Age, in which "single separate ownership" is precisely not "within reach of all."

Whitman's identification with the blurred boundaries of the lower middle class is remarkably consistent. At the age of twelve, Whitman was apprenticed to the respectable printer William Hartshorne, whom he recalled, in a *Brooklyn Daily Eagle* tribute in 1859, as always "observing all the decorums of language and action, square and honest, invariably temperate, careful in his diet and costume, a keeper of regular hours."[36] Whitman never gave up this commitment to lower-middle-class respectability, independence, and clean living. In his journalism of the 1840s and 1850s, Whitman declaimed the virtues of "independent manhood" as represented by a particular person with a liminal class location: "[a] worthy young clerk or just-established junior partner, perhaps a thriving mechanic."[37] In *Democratic Vistas* (1871), Whitman declares, "When I mix with these interminable swarms of alert, turbulent, good-natured, independent citizens, merchants, clerks, young persons . . . a singular awe falls upon me" (*PW* 2:388). The question we have to answer is whether Whitman's lower-middle-class location allowed him a critical vantage point on his society. For Whitman's hopes of participation in a democratic culture were staked on his gaining access to the free market and involved an ambivalent embrace of the market's potentials for self-making.

With his career as a journalist and editor stalled, Whitman in the early 1850s was busy "totting up invoices for building materials, paying bills, buying and selling quickly built frame houses." According to Paul Zweig, Whitman "liked to see himself as one of Brooklyn's regular men, a builder and businessman." Succeeding where his father had failed, Whitman profited from his speculative investments in Brooklyn's expansion enough to make a cash payment of $1,840 for a house on Ryerson Street.[38] "Song of Myself" reveals a Whitman seemingly caught up in the "market revolution," that confluence of internal improvements, expropriated land, rapid industrialization, and newly available credit that allowed a range of new goods and services—ready-made clothes, home furnishings, patent medicines—to flow to consumers in distant markets across the continent.[39]

The market revolution created the impression of a "fluid, expanding equalitarian society," a "national order of instinctive traders and shoe-string enterprisers in free pursuit of maximum returns."[40] But it also created a fully developed market society, along the lines suggested by C. B. Macpherson, in which "[e]xchange of commodities through the price-making mechanism of the market permeates the relations between individuals," a society in which "all possessions, including men's energies, are commodities," with everyone "potentially in movement up or down the scale of power and satisfactions."[41] The market society of Jacksonian America produced what Sacvan Bercovitch calls a "rhetoric of consensus," in which to be American was to be "self-made": "aspiring," "mobile," "adaptable," "unshackled by tradition."[42] Something of the force of this rhetoric, together with its admixture of inspiration and dread, of promise and risk, can be felt in the motto of the phrenologists Fowlers and Wells, who distributed Whitman's *Leaves of Grass*: "self-made or never made."[43] In its own way, Whitman's slim volume registers the ambiguities of this imperative.

"Song of Myself" is a poem governed by the dynamics of marketplace circulation, which Marx describes in 1867 as the process by which human labor is metamorphosed into the abstract form of the commodity. The "materials of nature," Marx writes, with their "sensuously varied objectivity as articles of utility" change into things that "transcen[d] sensuousness" when they emerge as commodities.[44] When they "assume the shape of values," Marx continues, commodities "strip off every trace of their natural and original use-value, and of the particular kind of useful labor to which they owe their creation, in order to pupate into the homogeneous social materialization of undifferentiated human labor."[45] The first survey of the commercial metropolis in "Song of Myself" provides a tactile sense of the labor performed in the artisan's workshop before its metamorphosis in the marketplace:

> The blab of the pave . . . . the tires of carts and sluff of bootsoles and talk
>   of the promenaders,
> The heavy omnibus, the driver with his interrogating thumb, the clank
>   of the shod horses on the granite floor [. . .]. (*LG* 31–32)

"Clank," defined by the *Oxford English Dictionary* as "a sharp abrupt sound, as of heavy pieces of metal . . . struck together," marks a ghostly, eruptive citation of labor, "the expenditure of human brain, nerves, muscles and sense organs," in the marketplace.[46] The occluded work of shoeing horses, cited earlier in a glimpse of the blacksmith's foundry ("[o]verhand the hammers roll—overhand so slow"), reemerges in the sound made by the progress of the omnibus in the crowded city street (*LG* 35).

But having taken an initial sounding of the market, the speaker of the poem commits himself to it and to its process of perpetual motion in noticeably more abstract terms:

> Myself moving forward then and now and forever,
> Gathering and showing more always and with velocity,
> Infinite and omnigenous and the like of these among them [. . .]. (*LG* 56)

Whitman identifies with the multitudinous acts of exchange he sees going on around him: what fascinates him is the dynamic movement of persons and things in the marketplace. Even as the "pure contralto sings in the organloft,"

> The quadroon girl is sold at the stand . . . . the drunkard nods by the
>   barroom stove,
> The machinist rolls up his sleeves . . . . the policeman travels his
>   beat. . . . the gatekeeper marks who pass [. . .]. (37)

Although these people are identified, what is striking is the way they recede
into their function as exchangeable units of labor—selling, nodding, rolling,
traveling, marking—in a homogeneous process of exchange. The predicative
structure of Whitman's catalog places each person in a relationship of perfect equality and perfect interchangeability. As Doris Sommer observes,
"the most extreme differences of social class, profession, origin, and gender
level out through the steady and ardent incantation that melts differences
into mere variation."[47] The commodity form is, Marx argues, "[a] born lev-
eller . . . always ready to exchange not only soul, but body, with each and
every other commodity."[48] Whitman catches not merely the "sprawling
vitality of modern life" but the energy of the marketplace, that space of
assembled particularity where differences of value are established and
resolved.[49]

The speaker of "Song of Myself" plunges into this space of motion and
exchange, identifying himself with it:

> What is commonest and cheapest and nearest and easiest is Me,
> Me going in for my chances, spending for vast returns,
> Adorning myself to bestow myself on the first that will take me,
> Not asking the sky to come down to my goodwill,
> Scattering it freely forever. (36)

Whitman announces that he is prepared to be a capitalist of the self, to
wager his spiritual capital, risking loss and failure in the expectation of "vast
returns." The question that arises is why Whitman should embrace the
market so enthusiastically. The answer, I think, lies in Whitman's earlier
political identity as a "Locofoco" Democrat and in its implied class location.

After learning his trade as a printer in Brooklyn, Whitman returned to
Suffolk County in 1838, purchased a handpress and fonts for fifty dollars,
and set up shop as "Walter Whitman, jun., editor and publisher."[50] After the
failure of his paper, the *Long Islander*, Whitman joined the Suffolk County

Democrat, which was allied to the Locofoco faction of the Democratic Party, a group of new men in business who resented the granting of special monopoly charters to corporations by state legislatures, as well as the reluctance of the banks to provide credit—factors that prevented ambitious craftsmen like Whitman from entering the market.[51] Their spokesman was William Leggett, chief editor of William Cullen Bryant's *Evening Post* and, later, of his own *Plaindealer*. For Leggett, the principles of laissez-faire—equal rights, free trade, minimal government—offered the best hope of success to "independent citizens, relying on their own resources for their prosperity" (*Leggett* 1:163). The role of government was "to give freedom to trade" and thus allow "enterprise, competition, and a just sense of public right" to accomplish happiness and prosperity through the supposedly natural operations of the market (2:326). Leggett's "steady and ardent incantation" of the virtues of the market was motivated precisely by the market's putative leveling of differences.

In his *Brooklyn Eagle* editorials of the 1840s, Whitman argues consistently for free trade, using the unabashed rhetoric of Manifest Destiny. "We free-traders are striking out in the mighty game of the world for our market," he declares on December 10, 1847, envisaging "distant kingdoms for our commercial tributaries!" (*GF* 2:64). Whitman made these arguments for free trade in goods, even while the deleterious effects of the free trade in labor were visible to him. In October of the previous year, he had lamented the condition of those "poor unskilled laborers" in the White Lead Factories of Brooklyn. "[O]pen to competition from anyone who has stout limbs," these workers had their wages cut by twelve and a half cents a day by the Factories' "rich. manufacturers" (1:156–57). But Whitman attributes the evils of the market to monopoly rather than competition. Free trade promises an extended liberty and a healthy corporate self, both national and individual. On April 20, 1847, Whitman was fully moved by the spirit of William Leggett, asking his readers to feel "this joy that among us the whole surface of the body politic is expanded to the sun and air, and each man feels his rights and acts them" (1:5–6).[52]

The preface to *Leaves of Grass* restates Whitman's laissez-faire position by explicitly linking the poetic and the economic: "The American bards shall be marked for generosity and affection and for encouraging competitors . . .

They shall be kosmos . . . without monopoly or secrecy . . . glad to pass any thing to any one . . . hungry for equals night and day" (*LG* 14). By evoking the emotional values of generosity, affection, and encouragement, Whitman spiritualizes the free market as a space that offers "the visible proofs of souls," a space of "perfect personal candour" where the soul can thrive and expand (14, 18). What enables the free development of the soul in the free market of souls is the "faith" and "candor" of visible "competitors," equals who meet and exchange spiritual capital night and day—just as, for Leggett, the market process is based on the "free exercise of confidence between man and man" (*Leggett* 2:334). What impedes this free development is "monopoly," the hoarding of spiritual and economic resources through "deceit or subterfuge or prevarication" (*LG* 18).

But Whitman is careful not to advocate too large a liberty, which would border on license and threaten anarchy. Instead, he recommends a revised notion of the "work-prudence-parsimony code," central to lower-middle-class identity.[53] Rather than see his fellow citizens strive only for "the independence of a little sum laid aside for burial-money, and of a few clapboards around and shingles overhead on a lot of American soil owned," Whitman urges a prudential action or "performance"—the soul accumulating and assimilating experience with "[e]xtreme caution or prudence, the soundest organic health, large hope and comparison and fondness for women and children, large alimentiveness and destructiveness and causality, [and] with a perfect sense of the oneness of nature and the propriety of the same spirit applied to human affairs" (*LG* 18). It is the oneness of nature and the homology of the natural with the social that underwrite this cautious enlargement and improvement of a self using its own organic resources. Again, Whitman follows Leggett, for whom the dynamic of the market is a "natural system," an irresistible, impersonal force with the "simplicity of nature" (*Leggett* 2:332, 334). Whitman declares his faith that "[a]ll that a male or female does that is vigorous and benevolent and clean is so much sure profit to him and her in the unshakeable order of the universe," where the profits will be both spiritual and economic (*LG* 20). He embraces market virtues redefined as spiritual attributes, which are deemed sufficient by themselves to redress the instabilities of the market, the deceits and subterfuges that result in monopoly.

This is the political philosophy of the group Richard Hofstadter defines as the Jacksonian "rising middle class," whose aim is "not to throttle but to liberate business, to open every possible pathway for the creative enterprise of the people."[54] Laissez-faire appealed to those attempting to make their way in the market against established players, to rise *into* the middle class: hence the mixture of radicalism and conservatism underwriting the adventures of the "party" of "farmers, mechanics, laborers, and other producers of the middling and lower classes" addressed by Leggett in their struggle against "the consumers, the rich, the proud, the privileged" (*Leggett* 1:66). This is a lower middle class with too much invested in the market to be able to imagine an alternative to it, a class pinning its hopes on the cleaned-up version its participation will ensure.

The hygienic metaphor is not a gratuitous one. In order to prosper on the basis of a "scanty fortune," the lower middle class need to be in good shape: all their physical and mental energies will have to be turned to good effect since their economic and cultural capital is relatively low.[55] In *Democratic Vistas*, Whitman makes this equation between health and economics clear. In the same way that the "human frame" is "best kept together by the simple miracle of its own cohesion," a diverse nation like the United States is "firmest held and knit by the principle of the safety and endurance of the aggregate of its middling property owners" (*PW* 2:383). In *Leaves of Grass*, Whitman's concern with "organic health" extends to a cautious refashioning of the conventional understanding of the "[u]rge and urge and urge" of sexual energy, linked to the economic by the metaphor of orgasm as "spending" (*LG* 26). But if Whitman's political-economic discourse represents his participation, body and soul, in the official Jacksonian doctrine of laissez-faire, his sexualized poetics reveal the darker side of that doctrine and a less expansive, more troubled conception of personhood.

The homology between sexual and capitalist economies was an established convention of Whitman's time, with the body imagined as a self-replenishing system whose vital powers were diminished by "excessive sexual indulgence" and enhanced by abstinence.[56] For the phrenologist Orson Squire Fowler, sexual activity creates an "excess of expenditure over supply," rendering "highly organized" systems "bankrupts of life."[57] For Fowler, and the majority of "male-purity" reformers, "self abuse" was particularly injurious. Its subjects are commonly "nervous, fidgety, easily agitated, fearful"; the masturbator is easily spotted by his or her personal "incoherence."[58] It is this homology of the sexual and the economic that allows Whitman's anxieties about life in the market—about "loss or lack of money" or "depressions or exaltations"—to be expressed in *Leaves of Grass* (28). The "grinding uncertainties, the shocking changes, the complexities and indirection" of life in a market society become cognate with the promptings and fluctuations of desire and its own internal economy of investment, expenditure, and exchange.[59] In Whitman's poetry, this relationship of the self to itself and to the market is dramatized through autoeroticism in a profoundly ambivalent practice of hoarding and spending.

Section 28 of "Song of Myself" describes masturbation in thoroughly conventional terms:

Is this then a touch? . . . . quivering me to a new identity,
Flames and ether making a rush for my veins,
Treacherous tip of me reaching and crowding to help them [. . .]. (*LG* 53)

The body is betrayed by its own sensory openness to experience. In a series of bizarre images, Whitman's senses both provoke and conspire against him, "straining the udder of my heart for its withheld drip," with "no regard for my draining strength" (53), until he becomes incoherent:

I talk wildly . . . . I have lost my wits . . . . I and nobody else am the
    greatest traitor,
I went myself first to the headland . . . . my own hands carried me there.
    (54)

Whitman follows the logic of what G. J. Benfield-Barker terms the "spermatic economy" in seeing masturbation as both a loss of self and the opening up of a division in the self, with reason betrayed by desire and the body's equilibrium lost.[60] The spermatic economy operates under the rubric of scarcity: sexual and economic resources must be husbanded carefully and used prudently. But, in an application of the principles of laissez-faire, Whitman extends the logic of the spermatic economy to make masturbation a prudential action in the kind of spiritualized free market established by the poem. In Whitman's revised scheme of things, masturbation is

Parting tracked by arriving . . . . perpetual payment of the perpetual
    loan,
Rich showering rain, and recompense richer afterward. (54)

Whitman adroitly combines two discourses, the economic and the natural, the one provoking anxiety and the other offering reassurance. "Spending," which refers to both production and consumption—the investing of sperm and capital and the exchange of bodies and goods—is a risky business. But the "pinings" Whitman has, "the pulse of my nights and days," provoke an anxiety that can be easily alleviated, since the cosmos itself spends freely and "[s]eas of bright juice suffuse heaven" (70, 50). The homology between nature and economy is licensed by laissez-faire, for which the free market is part of the natural order of things.[61]

This combination of heterogeneous discourses doesn't quite resolve matters, however. From one point of view, masturbation is fruitful and natural; from another, it places the body under an eternal debt or obligation, involving it in a process of treacherous enervation and discharge, "perpetual payment of the perpetual loan." Spending might be needful, healthful, obligatory, but keeping up the payments is a demanding business. Expenditure in *Leaves of Grass* is profoundly ambiguous, something to be celebrated but also regretted, even feared.

To be sure, spending in "Song of Myself" is typically imaged as healthful and procreative, sure of a return. Orgasm figures as the mark of a relation between the corporeal self and the object world that is mediated by a finely tuned nervous system: Whitman has "instant conductors" all over his body that "seize every object" and "lead it harmlessly" through him (*LG* 53). The world pours into the body, which matches its "procreant urge" with an expenditure of its own vital powers (26). Whitman hears "the trained soprano" and tells us that she "convulses me like the climax of my love-grip" (52). These urges and convulsions have an outcome that links national identity, poetic creation, and commercial success. While "jetting the stuff of far more arrogant republics," Whitman looks forward to the day when he will be "prodigious," receiving "puffs out of pulpit or print." Swearing on his "life-lumps," Whitman affirms that he is already "putting [him]self" to the "ambushed womb of the shadows" (71). A world still shadowy will become clarified and substantial once it has received the poet's inseminating words, the spendings of his "semitic [*sic*] muscle" (21).

But the poems that follow "Song of Myself," less often considered by critics, place this process of spending and return in a new context of doubt and risk. The poem later entitled "To Think of Time" introduces a note of anxiety by insisting, rather too strongly, that

> You are not thrown to the winds . . you gather certainly and safely
>   around yourself,
> [. . . . .]
> It is not to diffuse you that you were born of your mother and father—it
>   is to identify you [. . .]. (*LG* 102)

Spending seminal fluid means committing oneself to the "nebulous float" in the expectation of a return in the form of a zygotic "cohering," a process now shadowed by contingency as well as by a potential loss of self-coherence (104). Affirmation of the body's organic soundness, its potential for identification and merger with a host of other bodies, begins to turn into negation. This is particularly marked in "I Sing the Body Electric," ostensibly a hymn to physical perfection that becomes more concerned with "diffusion" than with a cohering "identity" when it comes to consider the "female form":

> Mad filaments, ungovernable shoots play out of it . . the response
>   likewise ungovernable,
> Hair, bosom, hips, bend of legs, negligent falling hands—all diffused
>   . . . . mine too diffused [. . .]. (119)

Spending has become "ungovernable," threatening the very self-identity and coherence it once guaranteed. The sane "human frame" underpinning the republic now becomes a random assortment of body parts, a body in pieces.

The speaker of "The Sleepers" finds himself "[w]andering and confused . . . . lost to myself . . . . ill-assorted . . . . contradictory" (*LG* 105). The healthy, freely-spending body now becomes vulnerable, lacking in coherence. The speaker cannot distinguish between the touch of darkness and that of a lover whose very presence is ambiguous, either that of a real person or the product of fantasy. "[W]hat was it touched me?" the speaker asks, having experienced not the punctual moment of spending but the fearful suspension of a desire that lacks an object and confounds the self. He wakes, "hotcheeked and blushing," a "foolish hectic" (107).

"Touch" functions here as the term that links the erotic and economic registers of Whitman's poetry. "Touch" connotes both endangered craft skill within the artisan economy and the dissolving sense of self-possession that results from physical contact or the desire for it. The lack of an object inciting and frustrating desire is cognate with the abstract relations of exchange that govern the market economy. The artisan works with the sensuous materials of nature, mixing his labor with his property in classically Lockean fashion to produce things that have tangible use-values. According to Edwin T. Freedley, describing manufacturing in the 1850s, early printers "made their own ink, as well as their type. This substance was applied to the letters or forms by balls made with sheepskin and stuffed with wool. With these one man *beat*, as it was called, the type, while the other laid the white or half-printed sheet on the tympan, preparatory to making the impression."[62] Artisanal labor involves what Elaine Scarry calls "sentient continuity between subject and object."[63] In Marx's words, "the instrument of labor" is still "intertwined with living labor."[64] In the market, this intimate connection between subject and object, worker and worked matter is sundered and replaced by the commodity-form, "a social relation between objects, a relation which exists apart from and outside the producers."[65] "I was chilled with the cold types and cylinder and wet paper between us," Whitman tells the reader in "A Song for Occupations," recalling his experience of wage labor as a typesetter in the mechanized pressroom of Park Benjamin's *New World* in 1841. "I pass so poorly with paper and types," he continues, "I must pass with the contact of bodies and souls" (*LG* 87). Whitman's experience of wage labor and mechanization is of an alienating abstraction of values that were formerly tactile and located in an immediate social context.

"Song of Myself" is replete with what Michael Moon describes as "quasi-sexual exchanges . . . fluid, oral, and seminal," through which Whitman espouses "boundary-dissolving experience."[66] "I fly the flight of the fluid and swallowing soul," the speaker declares; "I anchor my ship for a little while only" (*LG* 61). But the fluid medium of *Leaves of Grass* does not remain secure: images of an unmoored subjectivity drifting perilously come to predominate, and as they accumulate, they become increasingly linked to the marketplace.

In "The Sleepers," the speaker sees "a beautiful gigantic swimmer swimming naked through the eddies of the sea"—a man, like Whitman, "in the prime of his middle age" (*LG* 109). The scene at first recalls the erotic spectatorship of the upper-class woman, "souse[d]" with the "spray" of the twenty-eight bathers (34). But in "The Sleepers," the spectator feels hatred for the "swift-running eddies that would dash him headforemost on the rocks." He watches helplessly as the beautiful swimmer is "baffled and banged and bruised," until he is borne out of sight, a "brave corpse" (109). In "Morbid Appetite for Money," an *Eagle* article of November 5, 1846, Whitman condemns the get-rich-quick schemes of "visionary men" who "glitter for a moment—swim for a day on the tide of public favour—and then sink to a deserved and endless repose." He goes on to warn against speculative enterprises, "kept afloat solely and wholly by the fever for gaining wealth," and to urge the "great body of the workingmen" to "guard themselves" from the danger of launching themselves into such perilous waters (*J2* 103–4). In a traditional mercantile trope deriving from the eighteenth century, to suffer financial disaster was to be shipwrecked or drowned, an eventuality that also meant enduring a loss of manhood. Whitman's poetic imagery of a virile man unmanned by engulfing waters recalls both the economic and the sexual registers of his journalism.[67]

In the poem "Faces," among the "[f]aces of friendship, precision, caution, sauvity [*sic*], ideality," which pass in a "never-erased flow," are those of an "abject louse," a "milknosed maggot," and a face that is "an epilepsy advertising and doing business" (*LG* 124, 125). This last figure "falls struggling and foaming to the ground while he speculates well," as if in the grip of both psychic and market turbulence (125). These are the faces of "bosses," monopolists, landlords, "the agents that emptied and broke my brother"—an unwelcome reminder of the market's imperfections and excesses (125, 126). In "There Was a Child Went Forth," reality itself begins to dissolve with the dizzying speed of marketplace circulation. The speaker returns to the initial street scene of "Song of Myself":

> Men and women crowding fast in the streets [. . .]
> The streets themselves, and the facades of houses . . . . the goods in the
>   windows,
> Vehicles . . teams . . the tiered wharves, and the huge crossing at the
>   ferries;
> [. . . . .]
> The hurrying tumbling waves and quickbroken crests [. . .]. (139)

As he takes in the scene, the speaker wonders "[w]hether that which appears so is so . . . . [O]r is it all flashes and specks?" All the poem can affirm is that the objects of the "diffused float" are "part of that child who went forth every day"—a child who has no other identity than what he has witnessed, the distinction between subject and object now thoroughly broken down (139). The closing poem, "Great Are the Myths," affirms that "[t]he eternal equilibrium of things is great." All will be well in the cosmos of ultimate harmony, balance, and coherence—the natural order as a self-regulating market of souls, a kind of mutual fund of ill-defined returns. But what we have witnessed shows more of the "eternal overthrow of things" than their untroubled equilibrium (145). Values in the market economy, Marx notes, "vary continually, independently of the will, foreknowledge and actions of the exchangers." To be a worker in the market economy means being subject to "accidental and ever-fluctuating exchange relations," a nebulous float.[68] In the spheres of both production and consumption, Whitman is all at sea.

    The point I am making is not that we can read the sexual "as" the economic in *Leaves of Grass*, translating the terms according to an implicit hierarchy so that the economic is the "reality" and the sexual merely its figural substitute. Rather, Whitman's poetry dramatizes the economic as a system both social and corporeal, a general economy of expenditure and return that embraces the body as well as the social world. In this general economy, which is unabashedly capitalist, Whitman wants to spend freely and receive the vast returns due to him. But he is haunted by the suspicion that the market involves more "diffusion" than "cohering"—that to spend is not to gain but to lose oneself in a process marked by desire, fantasy, and loss.

In Whitman's ambivalent feelings about spending in this combined sexual-economic sense, we can see the beginnings of a cultural shift within the lower middle class, a transition from petty production and consumption to an anxious and conflicted engagement in mass production and consumption within the market economy. This shift was a widely noted feature of the Jacksonian period, in which, according to Melvin Meyers, "cool calculation" and "prudent pursuit of advantage" assume "the aura of an old-fashioned style." What we witness in *Leaves of Grass* is the evolution of a double personality, the "speculative enterpriser," with his "urgent quest for gain and advancement," emerging from his opposite, the "sturdy, stable citizen-producer"—twin personalities locked in a perpetual *psychomachia*.[69]

Whitman found a way out of these paradoxes and aporias: of a marketplace that is imperfect but all we have, of a body whose desires are both natural and unnatural, constantly shadowed and figured by the economic. His solution was to construct an eroticized class identity, based on an ideal of loving apprenticeship that maintains the lower-middle-class distinction of the honest artisan.

In the 1855 preface, the poet is a master craftsman who pursues his trade of enhancing souls in a free market guaranteed by the transcendent order of the cosmos, an order inimical both to the "cessation" of work among the urban underclass and to aristocratic "fatness and ease." He guides his readers in the same way a master craftsman guides his apprentice: "The touch of him tells in action. Whom he takes he takes with firm sure grasp into live regions previously unattained. . . . The companion of him beholds the birth and progress of stars and learns one of the meanings. Now there shall be a man cohered out of tumult and chaos . . . the elder encourages the younger and shows him how" (*LG* 22). The latent eroticism of the passage draws on a licensed daylight intimacy, the proximity of male bodies brought into chaste contact by hallowed patterns of labor and recreation. In his obituary tribute to the master printer William Hartshorne, Whitman remembers his "initiation" into the "pleasing mystery" of the "jour typo['s]" craft: "the half eager, half bashful beginning—the awkward holding of the stick—the type-box . . . put under his feet for the novice to stand on, to raise him high enough—the thumb in the stick—the compositor's rule—the upper case almost out of reach" (Brooklyn Printer 557).[70] It would be both anachronistic and redundant to identify passages like this with the "subterranean phallicism" of Freudian symbolism, coming as they do from an author who celebrates "libidinous prongs" and refers repeatedly to his own "semitic muscle."[71] Whitman is describing a powerful homosocial rite of passage that has its economic basis in skilled independent labor, the artisanal dream of earning a competency.

In "The Sleepers," Whitman applies the political economy of the artisan system to his own sensorium, personifying the senses that arouse him as "these journeymen divine." With his rational faculty as "their boss," he is immersed in their company and made "a pet" by them: "[o]nward we move, a gay gang of blackguards with mirthshouting music and wildflapping pennants of joy" (LG 106, 107). Whitman idealizes the artisan system to the point where its actual hierarchy is leveled and it becomes a utopian, communal form of production in which, in Terry Mulcaire's words, "productive activity becomes an aesthetic end in itself, where all activity occurs within the boundaries of a body whose scope and powers will have been enhanced in revolutionary fashion."[72]

Whitman longs for physical immersion in a "company" of male equals: a union in which, crucially, individual identity is preserved. In "I Sing the Body Electric," the speaker observes,

> The wrestle of wrestlers . . . . two apprentice-boys, quite grown, lusty,
>   goodnatured, nativeborn, out on the vacant lot at sundown after
>   work,
> The coats vests and caps thrown down . . the embrace of love and
>   resistance,
> The upperhold and underhold—the hair rumpled over and blinding the
>   eyes [. . .]. (LG 117)

Whitman's longing is so strong it presses key words into proximity as compounds ("goodnatured," "nativeborn") and merges separate elements into an unpunctuated whole ("coats vests and caps") while being tangible and overwhelming enough to blind the eyes. The speaker declares that

To be surrounded by beautiful curious breathing laughing flesh is
   enough,
To pass among them . . to touch any one . . . . to rest my arm ever so
   lightly round his or her neck for a moment . . . . what is this then?
I do not ask any more delight . . . . I swim in it as in a sea. (118–19)

This ideal form of sociability has the fluidity of marketplace exchanges
without the buffeting anxieties they generate, the equalitarian solidarities of
the artisan system without its restrictive hierarchy—without any of the
social ambiguities that separate the honest competency of the master from
the accumulating, exploitative activity of the boss. *Leaves of Grass* is
impelled, as Michael Moon observes, by a "homoerotic fantasy of [the] perfect 'fluidity' and 'specularity' of bodies and identities."[73] But this fantasy is
itself impelled by an idealized artisanal culture, all the more powerfully
cathected for being lost. The irony is that *Leaves of Grass* memorializes the
sexualized class identity that emerges from artisanal culture, while at the
same time paying an ambivalent tribute to the very market economy
responsible for that culture's destruction.

We would do well, I think, to read the Jacksonian enthusiasm for self-
making and the celebration of commerce as both willed and pressured, the
ideology of lower-middle-class citizens caught, in Judith Shklar's words,
"between racist slavery and aristocratic pretensions."[74] If there is a critical
edge to the first *Leaves of Grass*, it is to be found in the fraught, conflicted
state of mind induced by this dilemma rather than in any straightforward
ideological position. If Whitman's embrace of the market is ambivalent,
then that ambivalence leaves open the possibility that there might be alter-
natives to the market and the logic of the commodity. Glimpsed beyond
what James Livingston calls the market's "epistemology of excess" lies what
Jackson Lears describes as a "basic human need for a coherent, independent
identity, to be secured through satisfying, useful work"—a need that, in
Whitman, keeps surfacing through the rhetoric of laissez-faire.[75]

We also have to accept that Whitman's poetry registers the costs to the
lower-middle-class psyche of the market revolution, rather than forging
political bonds with its economic victims. Although Whitman, in his journalism of the 1840s, discusses the questions of waged labor and growing

inequality, which had tormented radical workingmen like Thomas Skidmore and liberal journalists like Orestes Brownson, he is silent on the subject in his poetry of the following decade.[76] The "shovel-handed Irish," the "[two] millions of paupers receiving relief," the "miserable factory population, or lazzaroni" that so appalled Emerson are conspicuously absent from Whitman's catalogs.[77] The political bonds Whitman does make in *Leaves of Grass* are with an already superseded artisan class and a slave population whose economic and political destiny is as yet unresolved.

"Song of Myself" begins with Whitman fleeing "[h]ouses and rooms" that are "full of perfumes," signaling his rejection of stuffy bourgeois culture (*LG* 25). But it's not long before a "runaway slave" comes to his own house. The runaway slave, with his "revolving eyes and his awkwardness," is depicted with a mixture of stereotype and sympathy, presenting a paradoxical image of nobility and abjection (33). But the episode highlights the material basis of Whitman's self-expression. He may "lead no man to a dinner-table or library or exchange," but his possession of a tub, a spare room, and "coarse clean clothes" stand in self-flattering contrast to the slave's utter lack of these commodities (80, 33). Whitman demonstrates, all too readily, that he is a worthy member of the producing lower middle classes, his intermediate position between aristocratic pretension and racist slavery heavily underscored. In his readiness to supply these credentials, as with his apparent enthusiasm for the market, Whitman testifies to what Jackson Lears calls "the enduring tension between coercion and release at the heart of market culture."[78]

On February 10, 1860, a letter was dispatched to Whitman from Boston:[79]

> DR SIR. We want to be the publishers of Walt Whitman's Poems— Leaves of Grass.—When the book was first issued we were clerks in the establishment we now own. We read the book with profit and pleasure. It is a true poem and writ by a *true* man.
>
> When a man dares to speak his thought in this day of refinement— so called—it is difficult to find his mates to act amen to it. . . . If you will allow it we can and will put your books into good form and style attractive to the eye; we can and will sell a large number of copies; we

have great facilities by and through numberless Agents in selling. . . .
([W]e do not 'puff' here but speak *truth*).

We are young men. We "celebrate" ourselves by acts. Try us. You
can do us good. We can do you good—pecuniarily. . . .

Yours Fraternally

THAYER & ELDRIDGE

Whitman's voice seems to have spoken to the men of the urban lower middle class. William R. Thayer and Charles W. Eldridge, "a pair of upstart
Boston publishers with abolitionist sympathies," went on to publish the
1860 edition of *Leaves of Grass* before going bankrupt during the Civil War.[80]
Their letter is self-consciously uncultured—a mix of the ungainly and the
assertive. Indeed, it engages in a polemical aside against "refinement—so
called." A truer refinement than that of Boston is, by implication, to be
found in the "acts" of honest men doing business with each other, in square
dealing and plain talk. There is a nod toward artisanal comradeship in the
implied promise that Thayer and Eldridge will fulfill the obligations of a
man's "mates" in the fraternity of entrepreneurial clerks. Whitman jumped
at the chance and agreed to 10 percent net of sales.

Whitman's ambiguous class location raises the question of the relationship between class and language. Thayer and Eldridge's letter reveals how
class works its way into a reflexive awareness of the linguistic medium, producing both a sense of bravado and a certain lack of fluency. The Boston
upstarts write as if uncomfortably aware of the implied presence of a refined
auditor hovering at their elbow, wincing at every solecism. What kind of language is available to a lower-middle-class poet of scant education and limited
cultural resources? What does one presume? And how does one begin?

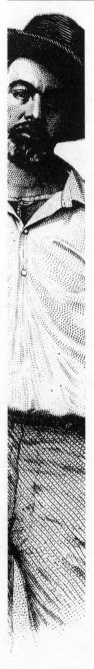

2 : THE AMERICAN 1848

I CELEBRATE MYSELF,
And what I assume you shall assume,
For every atom belonging to me as good belongs to you.

I loafe and invite my soul,
I lean and loafe at my ease . . . . observing a spear of
  summer grass. (*LG* 25)

So begins "Song of Myself," Whitman's extraordinary, and
extraordinarily presumptuous, poem. Leaving aside the
many layers of presumption for a moment, I want to draw
attention to a muted but nevertheless insistent conflict
between competing language systems in these opening
lines, a clash of tongues that reverberates throughout
"Song of Myself." These differences in linguistic register
form a central, if underacknowledged, part of what Whitman famously told Horace Traubel was his "language
experiment" (*AP* viii). They also relate to the political
conflicts in which the poem engages at a subterranean
level. The wager I make here is that a detailed explication
of the stratified layers of language that comprise "Song of
Myself" will force these conflicts into the light of day.

The first three lines of the poem are quite unremark-
able: the tone is relatively even, the diction formal and
Latinate. An educated reader of the mid-1850s would have
had little difficulty recognizing to "celebrate" and to
"assume" as literary language. That reader might have
been jarred somewhat by the starkly scientistic "atom"
arriving in the third line, but the specialized vocabulary of
chemistry was becoming more diffused as a result of the
antebellum interest in popular science. Whitman himself

had reviewed Justus Liebig's *Chemistry in Its Application to Physiology and Agriculture* (1847), made available in a "handsome new edition, by Wiley & Putnam, New York, for seventy-five cents," relaying to the *Brooklyn Eagle*'s readers the information that chemistry involved "the essences of creation," their "changes," their "growths," "formations, and decays" (*J2* 288). Perhaps another minor disturbance might have been felt in the passage from the lofty "I celebrate myself" to the blunt vernacular of "as good belongs to you," where a self-consciously "poetic" opening gives way suddenly to the curt, abrupt tone of someone bargaining in the street, anxious to clear away equivocations and clinch a deal. Since everyone in their corporeal being is composed of atoms, the speaker seems to insist, individuals are near enough equivalent to each other: we are all woven of the same essential stuff.

It's in the fourth line, though, that the trouble really begins for a reader of poetry accustomed to evenness of tone (and I will argue shortly that Whitman's readers would be so accustomed). To "loafe" (from the German *laufen*, to run) is a verb with an established vernacular usage. The noun, "loafer," meant, according to Webster's *Dictionary*, "[a]n idle man; a vagrant who seeks his living by sponging or expedients" and was heard originally in the New York markets. The word made an early appearance in print in 1835, in Cornelius Mathews's "The Late Ben. Smith, Loafer," the story of "a metropolitan loafer, and a phenomenon," who functions as the "ruling luminary of a whole shoal of shag-tailed comets that used to shoot madly about the terrestrial firmament of New York."[1] It gained major currency with the 1837 Panic and the depression that followed, when "loafing" became associated with the enforced idleness of mass unemployment.[2] To loaf, then, is not an expression that sits easily in a poem alongside high-flown talk of atoms and the soul.

An idea of just how high-flown this language was may be gained from Whitman's likely sources in Emerson and the Eastern mysticism that appealed to the Concord transcendentalists. In the *Eagle* for December 15, 1847, Whitman quoted a "striking paragraph" from "Spiritual Laws," which had appeared in Emerson's *Essays: First Series* (1841), reprinted that year. In reflecting on our past life, the quoted paragraph argues, we find that things "familiar and stale," as well as things "tragic and terrible," have a kind of "grace." Once it achieves this kind of detachment, "[t]he soul will not know either deformity or pain" (*J2* 281). Emerson's essay develops the idea that the "mechanical actions" of our merely social existence are not what counts in life: what counts is our natural "power" or "vital energy."[3] In perfecting ourselves, we should follow the calm superiority of "external nature," its "easy, simple, spontaneous action."[4] "The rich mind," Emerson says, "lies in the sun and sleeps, and is Nature." Loafing on the grass, Whitman invites his soul to join him with something of Emerson's delighted insouciance.[5]

But if they share a common concern for the health of the spirit, the linguistic register and social context differ significantly between the Concord sage and the Brooklyn house builder. Drafting what became "Self-Reliance," Emerson reached for "loafing" in a pejorative context to describe his theme's antithesis. "But now we are a mob," Emerson told his journal for March 10, 1839: "man does not stand in awe of man; nor is the soul provoked and admonished to stay at home in God; to root itself; & accept the whole of nature, the whole of history, the whole of thought; but it shuts its organs of reception & goes gadding abroad, a valet & a loafer."[6] For Emerson, "loafing" is inimical to the self-reliant soul in that it retains its political connotations: its association with the democratic mass, the servile, the unthinking.

What we are presented with in Whitman's opening lines is a set of alien languages, broadly constituted by the literary and the vernacular, jostling in uncomfortable proximity to each other. The jostling continues across the verbal surface of "Song of Myself" and was noticed by Whitman's first readers, who remarked on what they saw as disparity, disjunction, and division in the poetry. Charles Eliot Norton, writing in *Putnam's Monthly Magazine* for September 1855, found Whitman's poetry monstrous in its "self-conceit" and its contempt for "all usual propriety of diction." It nevertheless exerted a strange, contradictory appeal: "gross yet elevated," "superficial yet profound," "preposterous yet somehow fascinating," Whitman's language appeared to Norton as a "compound" or "mixture" of "Yankee transcendentalism and New York rowdyism" (*CH* 25). Somewhat nearer to home, the *Brooklyn Daily Times* judged Whitman's volume to be "[f]anciful" and "fertile," yet often "inelegant, and sometimes downright low," comprising "a multitude of oddities and excellencies."[7] Less charitably, the *Boston Intelligencer* described it as a "heterogeneous mass of bombast, egotism, vulgarity, and nonsense" (61).

F. O. Matthiessen, in *American Renaissance* (1941), continues this tradition of critical dissatisfaction. A particular source of annoyance for Matthiessen is Whitman's "odd habit of introducing random words from other languages," as when he salutes his "[e]lleves" (*LG* 69) or picks out from the urban crowd "one that shall be my amie" (56).[8] Whitman's "smattering of French" is evidence of his "ecstatic and monumental tastelessness," of his "confused American effort to talk big by using high-sounding terms" with only "the vaguest notion of their original meaning," evidence of the "happy pride of the half-educated in the learned term."[9] Matthiessen concludes that Whitman's diction bears no resemblance to a "folk-speech": "In its curious amalgamation of homely and simple usage with half-remembered terms he read once somewhere, and with casual inventions of the moment, he often gives the impression of using a language not quite his own."[10] Matthiessen wants Whitman to be a man of the people, speaking a natural language developed "by the slow absorption through every pore of the folkways of a single spot of earth."[11] Frustratingly, embarrassingly, Whitman turns out to be a lower-middle-class gate-crasher at the select soiree, grabbing clumsily and greedily at every cultural signifier he can lay his hands on; his *sermo vulgaris* smells distinctly of the lamp. What Gay Wilson Allen terms "the democratic 'mélange' which often resulted from Whitman's indiscriminate mixture of all levels of linguistic usage" has proved an abiding problem.[12]

Allen formulates an approach to this problem that has become influential, even central, in Whitman criticism. The approach involves an appeal to Emerson's "The Poet" (and is based on the understanding that Emerson can be safely said to speak for Whitman, as though Whitman was regularly ventriloquized by him). Nature, as Emerson demonstrates in the essay, "is a symbol, in the whole, and in every part." This means that "the distinctions which we make in events, and in affairs, of low and high, honest and base, disappear when nature is used as a symbol." The vocabulary of "an omniscient man," the studiously aloof transcendentalist, would "embrace words and images excluded from polite conversation"—as well, of course, as words and images included in it.[13] All of these diverse words and images are symbols of the ultimate reality of soul or cosmos, the unity that encompasses and ultimately orders diversity. "Whitman's propensity for inventorying the universe is," Allen avers, "evidence of his desire to know life—*being*—in all its details, the small and the mean as well as the great and the good."[14] It only remains to declare Whitman's poetry "cosmic, animistic, and democratic" to remove the problem of unseemly and disconcerting mixture and hold "roughs" and "cosmos" in one, all-encompassing embrace.[15]

Whitman's self-presentation in the preface to *Leaves of Grass* as "arbiter of the diverse," together with his links to Emerson, has misled critics into identifying the linguistic mixtures of the poetry as smoothly and unproblematically achieved—as presenting the image of an essentially harmonious democracy, a pluralist utopia. I want to argue just the opposite to this case for Whitman the cosmic synthesizer and to emphasize the unseemly and disconcerting aspects of Whitman's linguistic mixture of loafers and souls, a mixture that raises questions that, it seems to me, the "cosmic" case avoids confronting altogether. By forcing high and low into the same verbal space, is Whitman attempting to mediate between them, dissolving social conflicts through a panoramic, "democratic" embrace? Or is he heightening those very conflicts, pushing signifiers from opposite poles of the social divide together into a combustible intimacy? The answer, I think, is that "Song of Myself" both sharpens and ameliorates class conflict, raising the specter of antagonism and crisis one moment and banishing it the next.

The ambiguity is there in "Spiritual Laws," which I have been arguing acts as both a point of reference and a point of departure for "Song of Myself." Emerson advocates a kind of poised equanimity as an ideal of conduct. "Every man," he declares, "sees that he is that middle point whereof every thing may be affirmed and denied with equal reason"—whether he receives news of "the tin-pedlar" or of "the seraphim," of "low circumstances" or "the grandeurs possible to the soul."[16] Spiritual laws seem to function in accordance with the democratic mean. But Emerson's commitment to the "nearness or likeness of nature," to the natural affinity souls have for like souls, has the effect of reinforcing class division.[17] An undertone of elite distinction, both supported and menaced by the common, sounds throughout the essay. "There are graces in the demeanour of a polished and noble person, which are lost upon the eye of a churl," Emerson observes.[18] He goes on to develop this idea: "Introduce a base person among gentlemen: it is all to no purpose: he is not their fellow. Every society protects itself. The company is perfectly safe, and he is not one of them, though his body is in the room."[19] We needn't worry, in other words, about the servants. Evidence suggests that Whitman may have bridled at Emerson's tone of lordship. "Shrewd & wise reflections," he wrote in a note on *Essays: First Series*, "tinged with the library."[20] Emerson's sagacity is purchased, Whitman implies, at the cost of ivory-tower insularity.

As a lower-middle-class autodidact, Whitman sought to emulate Emerson's equanimity, while protesting all forms of snobbery and cultural exclusion. As we shall see, Whitman consciously drew from the languages stratified above and below him: the languages of elite, "high" culture and that species of the vernacular that found its way into the print culture of the antebellum period: the always already mediated and constructed vernaculars of the penny newspaper, southwestern humor, sensationalist fiction, and the popular stage.[21] Whitman attempts to construct a kind of middle linguistic register that would, using his own term from "Song of Myself," "filter" these diverse strata and defuse their tensions:

> You shall not look through my eyes either, nor take things from me,
> You shall listen to all sides and filter them from yourself. (*LG* 26)

Faced with the deluge of print, Whitman offers himself as a model for the discriminating common reader, one who is able to conduct away the linguistic superfluity of the age. But cutting across this improving literary project is the political crisis of the 1840s, which arises from the unprecedented territorial expansion of the United States and the reawakening of the controversy over slavery it entailed. This vital question lent a perplexing ambiguity to class conflict in the northeastern states in the 1840s, rendering it both latent and manifest.[22] It also made crossing cultural and linguistic boundaries in the way Whitman does in "Song of Myself" a politically fraught enterprise.

Class conflict was latent in the 1840s because every square mile of new territory in the West promised to relieve the pressure of overcrowding and competition in the Northeast, creating a farm or business and, potentially, an independent yeoman republic that would make the landlord, the capitalist, and the manufacturer redundant. Class conflict was manifest because, from the standpoint of the radical urban Democrat, slavery was the privileged instrument of both the Southern plantocracy and the Northern capitalists and manufacturers enriched by the southern crop, as well as being a potential source of competition to free, white labor. These tensions were coming to a head in the years from around 1847 to the early 1850s, when Whitman was making the notes he shaped into "Song of Myself." For a radical Democrat like Whitman, these were economic, political, and psychological tensions: the promise of boundless space for self-creation and individual liberty on the one hand, the overwhelming pressures of class antagonism and the threatened dissolution of the Union on the other. "Song of Myself" is written at an extraordinary pitch of loathing and expectation, of class hatred and cosmic optimism. Both impulses feed into a poem fabricated from the opposing languages of high culture and popular print, an opposition that is alternately exacerbated and smoothed over. But to trace the pattern we need first to locate these two currents of language more accurately in their class contexts.

––––––––

The circle of Lewis Gaylord Clark, editor of the *Knickerbocker Magazine*, comprised the heart of literary New York. Included in it were Frederick Swartout Cozzens, wine merchant and author of *Prismatics* (1853); Henry Breevort, descendant of an old-stock, Knickerbocker clan of landowners; Charles Astor Bristed, the Cambridge-educated grandson of John Jacob Astor and satirist of the "Upper Ten Thousand"; and Henry Cary, president of the Phoenix Bank. Dedicated to preserving literature as the province of the genteel amateur, these men asserted that the words and phrases "selected" in "good writing" should be "pure and genuine English, or such as have been incorporated into our literature by the practice of the best authors."[23] The English Augustans—Johnson, Pope, and Addison—served as the standard of linguistic purity. Politically, these men were "aristocratic" Whigs: they supported the tariff and the monopoly interests Jacksonian Democrats denounced as "special privileges." Culturally, they were conservative, Anglophile, and elitist, believing in the values of neoclassicism: "respect for tradition, distrust of social change, maintenance of time-tested cultural standards, and commitment to learned rather than popular modes of expression."[24] Together, the members of the Knickerbocker circle formed a compact, literary-mercantile elite, a "practically homogeneous upper class which felt itself competent to legislate, culturally, for other classes."[25]

Whether at Columbia or at Harvard the textbook for the neoclassical standard was the Scottish rhetorician Hugh Blair's *Lectures on Rhetoric and Belles Lettres* (1783). The cardinal virtues of prose for Blair were, first, perspicuity: the use of such words "as belong to the idiom of the language which we speak," in opposition to "words and phrases that are imported from other languages, or that are obsolete, or new-coined, or used without proper authority"; second, propriety: the selection of such words according to "the best and most established usage," in opposition to "vulgarisms, or low expressions"; and, third, precision: the "retrenching" of all "superfluities," "pruning the expression, so as to exhibit neither more nor less than an exact copy of his idea who uses it."[26] A specimen of neoclassical prose is provided by the young Ralph Waldo Emerson, who pleased his instructors at Harvard by writing that "[t]he hope opened to man's aspirations is a future life of retribution to which all the energies of rational creation look forward, promised by revelation and confirmed by adaptation and analogy."[27] This is self-consciously a language of "correctness and stiffness" rather than "suppleness and native idiom," a style that values instead "artificial, impersonal, and unidiomatic precision."[28] Neoclassicism cleaves to the "abstract and latinate" rather than the colloquial, its Latinity signaling "restraint and order."[29]

American poetry followed the same requirements of order and sanctioned usage. "At the present day," William Cullen Bryant declared, "a writer of poems writes in a language which preceding poets have polished, refined, and filled with forcible, graceful and musical expressions."[30] Paul Fussell observes that Bryant's early poetry proceeds with "scarcely a ruffle in diction," as if it had "emerged from a computer programmed with a Basic English for poetry."[31] The poems carefully follow the tradition of Augustan reflective poetry epitomized by Gray's "Elegy," in which "landscape images" combine with "philosophical musings" on the meaning of "mortality, humility, contentment," the whole presented in a voice possessed of dignity and decorum.[32] Bryant's "Thanatopsis" (1817) obediently reels off a set of well-worn epithets, with its description of "the pensive quietness" of the "venerable woods" and their "complaining brooks," and comes complete with a "rude swain" who treads the "sluggish clod."[33] "To a Waterfowl" (1818) asks its subject,

Seek'st thou the plashy brink
Of weedy lake, or marge of river wide [. . .]?

—a question one imagines was seldom asked in its Maine setting.[34] The incongruities produced by Bryant's commitment to a sanctioned, literary diction are particularly evident when he makes a rare attempt to comment on the contemporary urban scene in "The Crowded Street" (1843). The poem's "flitting figures" are only dimly realized, passing on their way to the abstractions of "toil," "strife," and "rest."[35]

Thy golden fortunes, tower they now,
Or melt the glittering spires in air?

the speaker asks of a "[k]een son of trade." Bryant is apparently concerned more with lofty inversion and standardized epithet than with rude actuality.[36]

The Federalist literati of the early republic had placed the vernacular out of bounds. To introduce innovations or "colloquial barbarisms" into the language was to introduce anarchy. John Pickering, Harvard professor of oriental languages and Greek, compiled a glossary of Americanisms with the express wish of stemming "that torrent of barbarous phraseology, with which the American writers threaten to destroy the purity of the English Language."[37] Pickering attempted to further this aim "by carefully noting every unauthorized word and phrase," faithfully logging all "deviations from the *English* standard."[38] These deviations included the notorious *lengthy* (for "long"), the ridiculous *to guess* (for "to suppose"), as well as foreign interlopers like *prairie* ("censured by the Edinburgh reviewers as a Gallicism"), English provincialisms like *gumption,* and "extraordinary" innovations such as *caucus* ("never used in good writing") and *slang-whanger* (a "noisy talker, who makes use of political or other cant, which amuses the rabble, and is called by the vulgar name of *slang*").[39] These words struck conservative Federalists and their Whig successors as intolerably coarse and low; this was not the language of Dr. Johnson but of the swinish multitude, the barbarians at the gate. The *Knickerbocker* told its readers that Pickering had identified "a formidable host of intruders," who have "invaded" the "purity" of the language and were to be "driven from the country by the combined exertions of American scholars."[40]

In New York City in the early 1840s, the aristocratic Whiggery and literary conservatism of the merchant elite were challenged by a group of Democrats who styled themselves "Young America." Led by Evert Augustus Duyckinck, the son of a prominent New York bookseller, this group launched an attack on the "self-elected critics" and "literary lacquey[s]" of the Knickerbocker set, accusing it of idolizing men of "wealth," "standing," and "respectability" and organizing "*conversaziones* and literary *soirées*" for the purposes of "caballing and scandal."[41] They set out to replace neoclassical elitism with literary nationalism: "the crowded life of [American] cities" would supersede Augustan idylls.[42] The way in which the speech of "the people" could be mobilized against elite Latinity for political purposes is brought out in an address to the New York City Democracy by Gansevoort Melville (Herman's older and initially more famous brother) on March 15, 1844, Andrew Jackson's birthday. Melville sarcastically granted the fact that the Whigs

> have the advantage of us plain-spoken democrats in scented hair, diamond rings, and white kid gloves—[roars of laughter,] in the language of compliment and the affectation of manner, and most particularly, in their style of dressing. If one of these exquisites wished to express the idea contained in the home-spun adage, "There is the devil to pay and no pitch hot," he would say, "There is a pecuniary liability due to the old gentleman, and no bituminous matter, of the proper temperature, wherewith to liquidate the obligation."[43]

As Eric Partridge observes, slang contains a strong element of satire. Slang "hits the nail on the head; eschews ambiguity and periphrasis, and is pointedly expressive," exhibiting a "gamin joy" in "breaking the canons of good taste."[44] If the hierarchy of languages—from underworld cant through slang and colloquialism to literary language—is a reminder that we live in a class society, then one of the political uses of slang is to react against the perceived "pedantry, stiffness, and pretentiousness" of the upper classes.[45] Gansevoort Melville's speech (which brought the house down) makes visible the antebellum class struggle in language as well as the political parameters within which Whitman conducted his "language experiment."

In the Democratic Party's national organ, the *United States Democratic Review*, W. A. Jones listed the "favorite topics of the Poet of the People":

"The necessity and dignity of labor, of endurance; the native nobility of an honest and brave heart; the futility of all conventional distinctions of rank and wealth, when opposed to the innate claims of genius and virtue; the brotherhood and equality of men."[46] Jones was forced to admit that, unfortunately, "the great Poet of the People, the world-renowned bard, the Homer of the mass, has not yet appeared."[47] Receptive to this message in Brooklyn, Whitman denounced the "perfect cataracts" of antirepublican "trash" imported into America, urging the *Eagle*'s readers on July 11, 1846, to be "more just to ourselves and our own good taste" (*J1* 463).[48] In this new inflection of a long-drawn-out struggle, national vernacular expression became the stake in a conflict between a ruling merchant elite and its professional, middle-class challengers.

Young America's literary productions fell somewhat short of the mark, however. While Jones hailed the future Homer of the mass, Cornelius Mathews offered his *Man in the Republic* (1846). "The Journalist" begins with a labored analogy:

As shakes the canvass of a thousand ships,
    Struck by a heavy land-breeze, far at sea—
Ruffle the thousand broad-sheets of the land,
    Filled with the people's breath of potency.[49]

The poem proceeds to develop a trite comparison between the "dark-eyed spirit" who produces "base disloyal lies" and the man who "scatters, wide and free" the "gold-bright seed of loved and loving truth," before advising, obscurely,

Hell not the quiet of a Chosen Land,
    Thou grimy man over thine engine bending;
The spirit pent that breathes life into its limbs,
    Docile for love is tyrannous in rending.[50]

The *North American Review* grimaced at Mathews's "forced, unnatural, and distorted expressions," reproving "a singularity of phrase at once crabbed and finical." Literary Boston regretted the "far-fetched epithets," at once "harsh and unmeaning" of a poetry deformed "by every species of bad writing."[51] Still inured in a neoclassical tradition he cannot quite master, Mathews's "vernacular" is a confected, literary device, his "people" observed from a distance rather than given an expressive voice. But if Young America's version of the vernacular was inadequate, other versions were available.

As a habitué of the Park Theater, the young apprentice Walter Whitman might have witnessed, in September 1833, a performance of *The Lion of the West*.[52] Nimrod Wildfire, the hero of the play, tells Percival, an English merchant and "distinguished member" of the aristocracy, of his triumph over a boatman on the banks of the Mississippi:

> Mister says he, I'm the best man—if I ain't, I wish I may be tetotaciously exflunctified! I can whip my weight in wild cats and ride strait through a crab apple orchard on a flash of lightning—clear meat axe disposition! And what's more, I once back'd a bull off a bridge. Poh, says I, what do I keer for that? I can tote a steam boat up the Mississippi and over the Alleghany mountains. . . . My name's Nimrod Wildfire. Why, I'm the yaller flower of the forest. I'm all *brimstone* but the *head*, and that's *aky fortis*.[53]

This figure, that of the "rhapsodic, crowing backwoodsman," was created out of the real-life exploits of Davy Crockett, the Tennessee frontiersman and sometime Democratic politician. Besides serving as a model for Nimrod Wildfire, Crockett became the hero of popular tales in the penny newspapers and almanacs.[54] Wildfire's extravagant brag was one means by which a subterranean current of popular speech rose to the light of day, capturing the "wild and lawless development of the language" happening "on the levels below the Olympians."[55] Among outlandish slang inventions, "cahoot," "catawampusly," "maverick," "roustabout," and "bugaboo" were added to the lexicon, along with the verb phrases "to fill the bill," "to light out," and "to cut a swathe." H. L. Mencken argues that, at its best, slang is not only "ingenious and amusing" but also embodies "a kind of social criticism."[56] But exactly what sort of social criticism can be derived from "the staccato gambolings of frontiersmen"?[57]

Nimrod Wildfire's creator, James Kirke Paulding, was a loyal supporter of the Jacksonian Democracy and drew on Crockett's native wit as a means of attacking Whiggish pretension.[58] The humor of Nimrod's outrageous talk depends on the polite frame of reference that encloses it, provided in this case by the gentleman Percival, whose smooth, educated accents jar against Wildfire's backwoods coarseness: Percival calls Wildfire "an amusing original," describes his victory over the boatman as "a renowned achievement," and translates "old Mississippi style" as "[s]ome mode once peculiar to the wildness of the region."[59] The audience's enjoyment of their dialogue derives from the repeated spectacle of incongruity.

This is the basic pattern of what became known as southwestern humor. But as James M. Cox observes, the humor's mechanism works by "putting enormous imaginative pressure on both the gentleman and the bumpkin." As humorists refined their comic technique, the gentleman became "more and more foppish and effete," while the frontiersman "threatened more and more to take over the narrative."[60] In the hands of a literary artist like Augustus Baldwin Longstreet, southwestern humor becomes an instrument of class critique, exposing the need of the refined for "violence and picturesqueness" in order to demonstrate their "moral superiority" over what they supposed to be the incorrigibly delinquent masses.[61] At the same time, writers like Longstreet trade on their audience's desire to escape from gentility and urban complexity by consuming tangy, dialect-flavored stories about "ring-tailed roarers." Southwestern humor treads what Cox describes as "the border between refinement and vernacular," keeping "an edge of refined perspective" between itself and the vernacular, while "using that edge to barter for literary audience approval."[62]

Whitman first explored these tensions between class registers in language during his 1848 visit to New Orleans, made after he had been sacked as editor of the *Eagle* for his opposition to slavery. Whitman contributed to the *New Orleans Crescent* a series of "Sketches of the Sidewalks and Levees," which follow the conventions of the genre by playing off literary language against the vernacular. The first sketch, which appeared in March 1848, is of "Peter Funk, Esq.," a man employed to raise the bidding at auctions:

Funk, like all other illustrious personages who have become so well known, as no longer to need the titulary soubriquet of *Mister*, was born and brought up—no one knows where: at least the information we have on this point is exceedingly uncertain and contradictory. Without, therefore, descending into the particulars of his early training and history, or minutely tracing up the rationale of cause and effect, by showing that a youth of moral proclivity will, in time, run into that species of moral gum-elasticity which goes to constitute the blood and bones of individuals, comprising his *genus*, we shall proceed at once, *in media res*, as the boys say at college, and make known to you, gentle reader, that Peter Funk is a young gentleman "about town" who holds the highly responsible office of by-bidder in a Mock Auction—being engaged to said work by the "man wot sells the watches." (*UPP* 1:199)

The portrait performs the same balancing act between the polite and the coarse as *The Lion of the West*, heightening the tension between the speech of "the boys at college" and the "man wot sells the watches." This linguistic standoff is all the more charged since it is through impersonation and the adoption of a smooth "volubility" that Funk's scam succeeds: "many are the green 'uns that are bit," the narrator tells us "by the 'persuasive speech' of the auctioneer" (*UPP* 1:201). The narrator's Latinate diction, with its "illustrious personages" and "titulary soubriquets," is ironically complicit with its subject. So, in Cox's words, does "the refined frame live off and prey on the energy of the vernacular."[63] But if it only needs a few words of the vernacular to deflate the pretensions of the elevated, the barrage of elevated diction is able, at the same time, to cow and oppress the lowly, to make them compliant participants in the auction. We are in a kind of deadlocked space, where politically charged conflicts have no way to be released except through humor, through the adoption of the kind of ironic edge that barters for the approval of the middle ground.

The basic problem of Whitman's situation, I think, is that he needs to draw from both of the classes he satirizes: he wants both the polish of the refined and the energy of the coarse, although these social extremes are equally repellent to him. They became more repellent still when the controversy over slavery forced the class divisions of New York into spectacular visibility. Whitman's response was to produce a new kind of poetry with a biting satirical edge, a poetry that outrages the neoclassical standard of the mercantile-literary elite in the crucial respect that it mixes vernacular and literary languages without respecting the boundary between them. Whitman's language experiment, in other words, was shaped by the political and economic circumstances of a particular historical moment: the American 1848.

The dispute over slavery reached a new crisis at the point when Europe was in the throes of proletarian revolution, a historical coincidence that has led to the "irrepressible conflict" over slavery being termed "the American 1848."[64] The assumption behind this designation is that nineteenth-century America bypassed class conflict and settled instead for a long-running and ultimately destructive conflict over its "peculiar institution." But the dispute over slavery was also a class struggle that pitted the interests of King Cotton and its retainers north and south against those who wanted to see America's newly conquered territories in the West remain open to settlement, rather than be turned into plantations. Whitman's involvement in the Free-Soil movement sharpened his awareness of class division at just the moment he was beginning his "language experiment."

In August 1846, David Wilmot, a Pennsylvania Democrat, introduced an amendment that specified that Congress could appropriate two million dollars to pay Mexico for its territory, provided that slavery was made unlawful on it. "I would preserve for free white labor a fair country," Wilmot declared, "a rich inheritance, where the sons of toil, of my own race and color, can live without the disgrace which association with negro slavery brings upon free labor."[65] Wilmot's free-labor ideology was motivated by a combination of racism and the fear of economic competition—the belief that, if the spread of slavery were not halted, then "the presence of the slave" would "exclude the laboring white man."[66] Free-Soilers depicted the contested territories of the Mexican cession in terms of a Jeffersonian ideal: the land should be free for the yeoman farmer and independent artisan, for what Thaddeus Stevens called the "middling classes," who were "the main support of every free government."[67] The Wilmot Proviso was blocked by the Senate, where the "three-fifths" rule meant that Southern senators exercised an effective veto on all legislative procedure affecting slavery.

The New York Democracy was the scene of bitter divisions over the Proviso, between radicals or "Barnburners," drawn from the state's small farmers and mechanics, and conservative "Hunkers," who represented its commercial and financial interests and were therefore favorably disposed toward slavery. Inevitably, Whitman was a Barnburner. In an *Eagle* editorial for September 1, 1847, "American Workingmen, Versus Slavery," he defined the issue of whether slavery should be extended to the newly conquered territories of the West in class terms:

> The question whether or no there shall be slavery in the new territories which it seems concluded on all hands we are largely to get through this Mexican war, is a question between *the grand body of white workingmen, the millions of mechanics, farmers, and operatives of the country*, with their interests, on one side—and the interests of the few thousand rich, "polished," and aristocratic owners of slaves at the South, on the other side. (J2 318)

Understanding why slavery was a class issue in New York means grasping the extent to which New York's aristocracy, both Whig and Democrat, was implicated in the southern trade.

The plantation system of the South required northern capital to make it work. Southern wealth, concentrated in the hands of three or four thousand families, was tied up in slaves and land. The credit these planters needed had to come from elsewhere, and it came principally from New York's brokering, selling, banking, and insurance houses. New York–owned ships sailed from New Orleans to Liverpool loaded with raw cotton and returned to New York with British manufactured goods, which, to complete the "Triangle," they transported down to the South in exchange for more of the crop. New York capitalists funded southern mining and railroad ventures and became de facto slave owners when southern creditors defaulted.[68] By 1851, cotton made up 40 percent of America's exports, but forty cents of every dollar earned was taken by New York.[69] In 1855, the American Anti-Slavery society asked rhetorically what northern merchants meant when they said they desired the preservation of the Union and answered,

> They mean the clipper ships, Government contracts, warehouses bursting with merchandise, large profits, great dividends; they mean houses in Fifth Avenue or Beacon Street, services of plate, servants in livery, Potiphar Balls, dinners of seven courses and twenty-five kinds of wine, fine carriages and horses; they mean tours of Europe, winters in Paris and Rome, summers in Switzerland, presentations at court, tuft-hunting, and

toadying, purchases of pictures, books, statues—whatever, in short, money can buy.[70]

While the hard-pressed mechanics of Brooklyn and the Lower East Side dreamed of the free lands of the West, the merchants, bankers, and insurers of Manhattan placed their bets on slavery.[71]

The Free-Soil campaign of 1848 thus revived Locofoco agitation against the "aristocracy," which now included both "grasping bankers" and "aggressive slaveholders."[72] In the *New York Evening Post* for April 27, 1848, William Cullen Bryant declared that "a few slave owners" were "as powerful at the south and west as the manufacturers at the east."[73] In making their case against aristocracy and concentrated power, the Free-Soilers borrowed from the abolitionist cause the concept of the "Slave Power," first used in 1839 by an Ohio Jacksonian, Tom Morris, who had called on "the people" to wage war against "these two great interests—the slave power of the South, and banking power of the North—which are now uniting to rule this country."[74] In a speech of June 28, 1848, the "Conscience" Whig Charles Sumner denounced the "unhallowed union" of "the cotton-planters and flesh-mongers of Louisiana and Mississippi and the cotton spinners and traffickers of New England," an unholy alliance between "the lords of the lash and the lords of the loom."[75] For Free-Soilers and abolitionists in the American 1848, the class lines were clearly drawn.

Whitman's Free-Soil position cost him both his editorial post and his place in the New York Democracy. On November 3, 1847, in the wake of an electoral defeat by the Whigs, Whitman urged the *Eagle*'s readers to stay true to the Democratic "high radical doctrine," declaring that "all conservative influence is pestilential to our party." The "plague spot of slavery, with all its taint to freemen's principles and prosperity" must be allowed to spread "no *further*" (*J2* 347). Unable to toe the Hunker party line any longer, on January 13, 1848, Whitman denounced New York's Senator Dickinson for being "against Wilmot!" and was sacked by the *Eagle*'s Hunker owner, Isaac Van Anden.[76] After Taylor led the Whigs to victory over a split Democratic Party in 1848, his hopes for a political career within the New York Democracy were dashed. In June 1849, Whitman was the first to nominate Senator Thomas Hart Benton of Missouri for the presidency, anticipating the prospect of a sinecure after a Democratic victory led by a Wilmot supporter. But in September Hunkers and Barnburners ran a joint ticket for the sake of party unity. Whitman promptly resigned the editorship of a party newspaper, the *Freeman*, where he had taken refuge after the *Eagle* debacle, and was hounded out of the Seventh Ward by party henchmen loyal to the Hunker cause. He found himself "the butt of derisive analysis" in the press, tinged with class condescension, the *Brooklyn Advertiser* describing him as "a civilised but not a polished Aborigine," the *Eagle* as the "shirt collar man."[77]

Without an editorship and without a party, Whitman had no way to pursue the cause of Free-Soil or to protest against the Compromise of 1850, in which thirty-five Northerners led by Daniel Webster yielded to the South's demand for a tougher fugitive slave law. "[I]n this critical season of political flux, realignment, and threat of dissolution of the union," Whitman wrote a series of letters to the Sunday *Dispatch*, in which a strong class animus breaks through. The "great body of 'fashionables,'" around the "aristocratic neighborhood" of Union Square, he observed, were "vulgar, flippant and overweeningly selfish."[78] As principal editor of the penny *Daily News*, Whitman "objected to carriages' forcing omnibuses off Broadway, for the street belonged to all classes and it was a gross injustice to surrender to a monopoly of the aristocracy; a laundress or seamstress laden with bundles had as much right to walk there as the lady driving home with a thousand-dollar shawl purchased from Stewart's or Beck's."[79] These upper-class slights were aspects of what Whitman called "the questions at issue between the Slaveocracy and the rest of the American people."[80]

In the early months of 1850, Whitman contributed a series of poems to Bryant's *Evening Post* and Horace Greeley's *Tribune*. "Song for Certain Congressmen," which appeared in the *Evening Post* on March 2, begins as follows:

We are all docile dough-faces,
    They knead us with the fist,
They, the dashing southern lords,
    We labor as they list;
For them we speak—or hold our tongues,
    For them we turn and twist. (*EPF* 44)

The opening line is glossed by an epigraph from Webster's *Dictionary*, "like dough; soft; yielding to pressure." Bartlett supplies the 1848 definition of "dough-face": "[a] contemptuous nickname, applied to the Northern favourers and abettors of negro slavery. Generally it means a pliable politician,—one who is accessible to personal influences and considerations." "Dough-facism," in short, meant "truckling to the slave power."[81] Clear signs of a new strain within Whitman's Augustan poetic diction emerge in this, the first of a series of poems he published in 1850. The political slang of "dough-faces" clashes with the conventionally poetic "we labor as they list"; the Latinate rhymed words begin to buckle under the strain of a contemporary political discourse admitted into the poem in quotations:

> To put down "agitation," now,
>> We think the most judicious;
> To damn all "northern fanatics,"
>> Those "traitors" black and vicious;
> The "reg'lar party usages"
>> For us, and no "new issues." (*EPF* 44)

Judicious, vicious, new issues: the declension, if forced, makes its point by being jarring and abrupt. The next poem, "Blood Money," in the *Tribune* supplement for March 22, abandons rhyme in favor of a biblical denunciation of Daniel Webster's notorious Senate speech supporting the Fugitive Slave Act:

> Curs'd was the deed, even before the sweat of the clutching hand grew
>> dry;
> And darkness frown'd upon the seller of the like of God. (47)

Whitman next contributed "House of Friends" to the *Tribune* on June 14, turning to irony:

> Arise, young North!
> Our elder blood flows in the veins of cowards—
> The gray-haired sneak, the blanched poltroon,
> The feigned or real shiverer at tongues. (37)

The irony consists in playing off the lofty "elder blood" against the emphatically low "sneak" (cant for "petty thief"; generically, all thieves and swindlers) and the more literary "poltroon," adding a further twist by giving each curse word its own dainty poetic epithet.[82] "Resurgemus," which appeared in the *Tribune* on June 21, repeats the trick but with a more elaborate clash of language systems. The poem begins in the manner of Blake's prophetic, mystic-revolutionary visions, complete with biblical reference:

> Suddenly, out of its sta[l]e and drowsy [l]air, the [l]air of slaves,
> Like lightning Europe le'pt forth,
> Sombre, superb and terrible,
> As Ahimoth, brother of Death. (38)

While we're considering looking up Ahimoth—a Levite priest, son of Elkanah, the father of the prophet Samuel (1 Chronicles 6:25)—the second stanza breaks into an abrupt vernacular interjection:

> God, 'twas delicious!
> That brief, tight, glorious grip
> Upon the throats of Kings. (38)

Here, Whitman is not just "ushering the idiom of working-class reformers into poetry" but confronting the high with the low in a linguistic patterning filled with class tensions.[83]

As a literary genre, southwestern humor erects a kind of cordon sanitaire around popular speech. The framing device of the genteel narrator relaying the vernacular controls its energies and distances its threat. The two voices are clearly separated and kept separate: they must not be allowed to mix. This is not the case in Whitman's poems of 1850. Whitman appropriates the literary language of the mercantile-literary elite and turns it against them; this accounts, I think, for the curiously double-voiced aspect. Whitman elevates his own language through trying on a high literary register, descending to the vernacular to point out that this performance contains an element of irony and masquerade. To steal this language is to gain a grip on the throats of kings, a grip that, once obtained, can relax back into the vernacular. The abrupt and indeterminate transitions between languages in themselves involve a flouting of the neoclassical standards of perspicuity, purity, and propriety—and, by extension, the class rule of the elite responsible for their maintenance. When he comes to write "Song of Myself," Whitman holds on to this practice of weaving political confrontations into the linguistic texture of the verse. The political tensions that provoke the 1850 poems are not defused; when Whitman begins publishing poetry again in 1855, the abhorrence has scarcely dissipated. But Whitman's specific class grievances cohabit uneasily with an impulse toward the bardic celebration of American possibility, an ambivalence that is deeply embedded in the historical moment of the 1840s.

Throughout the 1840s, territorial expansion provoked class conflict, only to mask and displace that conflict with the image of open space and social mobility. The genealogy of the concept of manifest destiny, as elaborated by the New York lawyer and radical Democrat John O'Sullivan, follows this pattern. O'Sullivan's early concerns as editor of the *Democratic Review* in the early 1840s were with political economy and morality, specifically with "relative poverty" and the "unequal distribution of wealth."[84] O'Sullivan describes the "revolting bondage" of the "*White Slave* of the factory and of the coal-mine," whose degradation is "the immediate consequence of undue privileges—of undue obstacles to the free circulation and natural reward of labor."[85] In New England's manufacturing districts, "thousands of destitute females passively submit to all the horrors and privations of the factory system," a system that produces a "multitude of defective beings, with sallow complexions, emaciated forms."[86]

By 1844, O'Sullivan had hit on a possible solution to the problem of the degradation of industrial workers who command "less wages, as population gradually fills up the market of labor."[87] Close by the urban population of the Northeast lies "the safety-valve of the public lands."[88] When New England's workers feel "the iron hand of competition" pressing "too harshly upon them," they might, therefore, be allowed to escape "to the free woods and rich lands of the Far West."[89] Like other Democrats in the 1840s, O'Sullivan seizes on territorial expansion as what Thomas R. Hietala calls an "antidote to the toxins of modernization."[90] For O'Sullivan, the settlement of the West provides an opportunity to reinfuse the Jeffersonian ideal of an independent yeomanry into the republic, a means of securing "free circulation" and "natural reward."[91]

The annexation of Texas in the following year inspires O'Sullivan to coin his famous phrase. In a December article for the *New York Morning News*, O'Sullivan asserted "the right of our manifest destiny to overspread and possess the whole continent which providence has given us for the development of the great experiment of liberty and federated self-government."[92] From this point onward in the 1840s, political economy is superseded in the public discourse on expansion by what Anders Stephanson calls "geopolitical prophecy."[93] Dynamic capitalist expansion becomes fused with a Christian vision of nature as the "providential configuration of space on earth" and a new, geophysical description of the North American land mass.[94] Faced with the grimy realities of urban development and the actual violence involved in taking land from Mexicans and native peoples, destinarians of all kinds gloried in the spectacle of the continent, in what the geographer Arnold Guyot hailed as "the simplicity and grandeur of its forms, the extent of the spaces over which it rules."[95] According to a peculiarly circular logic, a vista this magnificent could only have been destined for democracy and capitalism. Positive science reveals America to the expansionist gaze as "the theatre, seemingly arranged by Him for the realization of the new social order, towards which humanity is tending with hope. For the order of nature is a foreshadowing of that which is to be."[96]

Whitman's *Brooklyn Eagle* editorials of the mid-1840s stick closely to the religious, scientific, and political dimensions of Manifest Destiny as measured by O'Sullivan. "The scope of our government, (like the most sublime principles of Nature), is such that it can readily fit itself, and extend itself, to almost any extent," Whitman declares on May 11, 1846 (*GF* 1:242–43). On June 23, he detects the hand of Providence: "[w]e look on that increase of territory and power—not as the doubter looks—but with the faith which the Christian has in God's mystery" (*J1* 434). A July 28 editorial headed "Swing Open the Doors!" echoes O'Sullivan: "[w]e must be constantly pressing onward," Whitman urges, "carrying our experiment of democratic freedom to the very verge of the limit" (481). By November 24, Whitman is dilating on "American Futurity," anxiously anticipating the "holy millennium of liberty," and indulging himself in a moment of panic about the consequences "[i]f it should fail." "O, dark were the hour and dreary beyond description the horror of such a failure," he writes, before hastily resuming the patriotic register by adding that such a failure is to be anticipated "not at all" (*J2* 133). On December 16, any misgivings about the violence involved in expansion are banished in approving the "most bloodless" war "ever known on earth!" The Mexican War is, moreover, a war fought in the name of democracy and freedom: "[w]e love to record these things, because we love to record all signs of ameliorated humanity" (150). The new contours of the American empire attained a spectacular visibility before Whitman's eyes when, on the night of April 16, 1847, a patriotic crowd of Brooklynites gathered around the *Eagle* office building. According to Whitman's account, "[a]t a given signal" the front of the building was changed "from total darkness to a blaze of light. A transparency, inscribed with the now historical names of PALO ALTO, RESACA DE LA PALMA, MONTEREY, BUENA VISTA, AND VERA CRUZ, shone clearly from the second story, and evinced to the multitude in front the reason of the proceeding" (246). All contradictions and doubts have, it seems, been resolved by an appeal to cosmic harmony, a nation's divinely appointed rendezvous with destiny.

A very different set of preoccupations emerges in the "Talbot Wilson" notebook, in which Whitman experimented with ideas and free verse lines that would be incorporated into "Song of Myself."[97] In this notebook Whitman struggles to reconcile his deep-seated sense of class division with the role of bardic poet of Democracy, as scripted for him by the prophets of Manifest Destiny and Young America. Whitman begins "Talbot Wilson" by adopting the tone of both O'Sullivan and Duyckinck. The first extant page reads: "True noble expanding American character is raised on a far more lasting and universal basis than that of any of the characters of the 'gentlemen' of aristocratic life, or of novels, or under the European or Asia[tic] forms of society or government.—It is to be illimitably proud, independent, self-possessed generous and gentle." Whitman tells himself that, as an American, he is as good as anyone and will "accept nothing except what is equally free and eligible to any body else" (*TW* 17). But the assertion of this "true" equality is made precisely because Whitman is conscious of social hierarchy, the practice of dividing men "like metals" into "those more precious and others less precious, intrinsically." His conviction of equal worth is so profound that these reflections continue over four pages. Whitman is horrified by the prospect of experiencing "how it felt to think I stood in the presence of my superior." He vows that even if "the presence of God were made visible immediately" before him, he "could not abase" himself (20). Later on, he adds the thought that if he were to walk with God in heaven and God were to "assume to be intrinsically greater than I," he would "certainly withdraw from Heaven, for the soul prefers freedom in the prairie or the untrodden woods" (60).

Pursuing this Emersonian train of thought, Whitman arrives at a definition of his role as poet. Every soul has "its own individual language," but no two souls "have exactly the same language" (*TW* 35). The "great translator and joiner of the whole" is the poet, who "[h]as the divine grammar of all tongues, and says indifferently and alike How are you friend? to the President in the midst of his cabinet, and Good day my brother, to Sambo, among the hoes of the sugar field, and both understand him and know that his speech is right" (36). The language of the spirit serves to defuse political tensions, dissolving them in the embrace of "[t]he universal and fluid soul" (37). Whitman offers poetry as a cohesive force in a divided society, telling another notebook from this period that what is required are not "inquiries and reviews" but "satisfiers, joiners, lovers." Through such mediating figures, the "heated, torn, distracted" times are to be "compacted and made whole" (*NUPM* 1:96).

A class society, however, cannot be wished away: it persists and forces choices to be made. "I am hungry and with My last Dime get me some meat and bread, and have appetite enough to relish it all.—But then like a phantom at my side suddenly appears a starved face, either, human or brute, uttering not a word." The wordless phantom represents the guilt of the fortunate who know but cannot admit to themselves that they live under conditions of structured inequality: its uncanny appearance marks the return, from the outside, of the repressed. Whitman decides that, confronted with a greater need, it makes no sense "to talk of mine and his" (*TW* 50). From now on, Whitman's tone becomes sharper, the writing more specific in its critique: "The ignorant man is demented with the madness of owning things—of having by warranty deeds and court clerk's records, the right to mortgage, sell, give away, or raise money on certain possessions.—But the wisest soul knows that no object can really be owned by one man or woman any more than another" (52). Emersonian transcendentalism is joined with

Locofoco political sentiment—a statement of the most convinced and profound idealism. On the next page Whitman inveighs against anyone "who would grab blessings to himself, as by right, and deny others their equal chance" (53). Still haunted by the starving phantom, Whitman goes on to denounce "the dismal and measureless fool called a rich man," who "leaves untouched" those "spread tables thick in immortal dishes, heaped with the meats and drinks of God" (56).

Fully engaged now by the problem of class division and the choices of identification and sympathy that life in a class society imposes, Whitman makes a key decision. To be "illimitably proud, independent," and "self-possessed" means refusing to have anything to do with so-called social superiors, whether they be God walking in heaven or those "genteel spirits" who insist Whitman remove his "bristly beard" with "washes and razors" (*TW* 62). "I will not descend among professors and capitalists,—I will turn up the ends of my trowsers around my boots, and my cuffs back from my wrists, and go with drivers and boatmen and men that catch fish or work in the field. I know they are sublime" (65). Whitman refuses the genteel blandishments of the upper strata for the sublime coarseness and vitality of the lower—a decision abbreviated in "Song of Myself" to "Washes and razors for foofoos . . . . for me freckles and a bristling beard" (*LG* 46). "Foofoo" means, according to Mose in *A Glance at New York*, "an outsider . . . a chap wot can't come de big figure": an upper-class exquisite who belongs to Broadway rather than the Bowery (Baker 180).[98] But this decision is not made in "democratic" innocence as a gesture of inclusiveness or in benign tolerance of "diversity." It is made using a muted but still insistent vocabulary of class struggle and class abuse, the inheritance of both Locofoco and Free-Soil campaigns, with their repeated barbs against foppish Whigs, docile doughfaces, the slavocracy, "the rich, the proud, the privileged" (*Leggett* 1:66).

Two blank pages follow in the notebook. Then, abruptly, the theme of the bardic "joiner" returns. Only now Whitman has begun writing rough, uneven lines of free verse:

I am the poet of the body
And I am the poet of the soul
I go with the slaves of the earth

> equally with the masters
> And I will stand between
>   the masters and the slaves,
> Entering into both
> so that both shall understand
> me alike. (*TW* 68)

Mediator and ameliorator, universal translator of the soul's language—the fluid cadence of the lines gives a biblical sanction to the role of the poet in a democratic, albeit divided, society. But a few pages later, after Whitman has drafted the "Is this then a touch?" section of "Song of Myself," the tone changes again. "It were easy to be rich," Whitman writes across the top of the page, "owning a dozen banks." "It were easy to shine and attract attention in grand clothes[.] But to outshine in sixpenny muslin?" (94). Disgust and division break up the rhapsody: the woman in sixpenny muslin joins the starving man from Whitman's political unconscious. Whitman reaches out in democratic embrace of the nation but finds himself appalled by what such an embrace contains. It might be only chance that has resulted in Whitman writing in his notebook "*I am the poet of Equality*" immediately below a possibly earlier notation: "Amount rec'd from Mr. V. A. 1847" (83). But if "Mr. V. A." is Isaac Van Anden, who sacked Whitman from the *Eagle* for his Free-Soil apostasy and is apparently settling accounts with his disgraced former editor, then the palimpsest makes a historical point. The class of capitalists and professors to which Van Anden belongs continues to dine well on the profits of slavery. Whitman takes the money and writes "I am the poet of Equality." It sounds like a bardic announcement but also like a curse: a way of cleansing the mouth of a bitter taste.[99]

This tortured pattern of bardic celebration and class abuse is reproduced in "Song of Myself," which cannot shake off the grimmer musings of the notebooks from which it emerged—cannot quite free itself from the destitute females and defective beings produced by industrial capitalism. I will argue, in the next chapter, that the poem's rhetoric of manifest destiny is continually inflected, and unbalanced, by the language of class. Liberty extended through space forms a kind of idealized and idealizing screen on which uncanny forms of degradation and conflict continue to emerge into visibility, as though from some repressed material base, only to be covered up again by the soaring vista. This oscillation between the spectral manifestation of class and its return to a latent, idealized form establishes the pattern of the poem, which is continually exacerbating then smoothing over the tension between the high and low linguistic currents feeding it. "Song of Myself" emerges from a particular historical moment in which Whitman is *both* Locofoco Democrat *and* epic poet-as-destinarian. Whitman's problem is that, like another of his contemporaries, he can never "quite make up his mind how to situate structural injustice" within what seems to be "a progressive-historical frame of American development."[100] The hesitation forms the political precondition for the poem's indeterminate, experimental texture, as well as its mixed impulses to praise and to blame. Both are the inheritance of the American 1848.

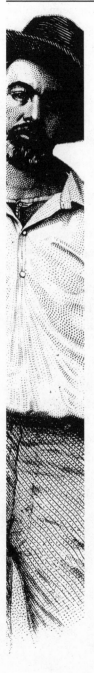

He leaves houses and their shuttered rooms, for the open air.
He drops disguise and ceremony, and walks forth with the
confidence and gayety of a child. For the old decorums of
writing he substitutes his own decorums. . . . [T]he rules of
polite circles are dismissed with scorn.

> Whitman, unsigned review of *Leaves of Grass*,
> *United States Democratic Review*, 1855 (*CH* 37)

You shall go in some rich man's house, where the long suite
of parlors has been attacked and taken possession of by
artists, ornamenters, makers of carpentry, marble mantels,
curtains, soft seats, and morocco binding for books.—What
can be unbrought; for the place yet looks very beggarly. The
gentleman who footed the bills, has surely forgotten
something.

> Whitman, 1854 notebook (*NUPM* 1:134)

It would be as though some publisher should reject the best
poems ever written in the world because he who brings them
to be printed has a shabby umbrella, or mud on the shank of
his boot. . . . One grand faculty we want,—and that is the
power to pierce fine clothing and thick coated shams, and
settle for sure what the reality of the thing clothed and
disguised is, and what it weighs stark naked; the power of
slipping like an eel through all blandishments and graspings.

> Whitman, notebook (*NUPM* 1:112)[1]

Whitman's notebook entries indicate the class animus
motivating the opening transcendental sections of "Song
of Myself." To recap those sections, the speaker tells us he
will celebrate himself and, in doing so, celebrate us, his

readers, since we are one in the equal distribution of atoms. He loafs, invites his soul, and observes a spear of summer grass. The scene shifts from the outdoors to the overrefined interior, houses and rooms full of perfumes. The speaker likes the fragrance, which would intoxicate him, but he will not let it. Instead he flees to the riverbank to become "undisguised and naked" (*LG* 25). He celebrates his body in a torrent of compound nouns: loveroot, silkthread, crotch and vine. There are shadowy presences of other figures, less densely embodied than the speaker: a few light kisses, a few embraces, a reaching around of arms. All this is offered as an experience of a reality more vital and sustaining than that of the perfumed salon, the speaker promising that if we join him by the riverbank, we will no longer takes things at second or third hand, look through the eyes of the dead, feed on the specters in books.

What is missing from the rich man's house is pith, substance, reality—in short, soul. The encompassing structures of finance capitalism, with their mortgages and bonds, libraries and paintings, conceal a spiritual vacuum and spread a pervasive unreality. The possessions of the rich are mere husks. Whitman's transcendental faith is that "[t]he kernel of every object" that can be "seen or felt or thought of has its relation to the soul, and is significant of something there" (*NUPM* 1:135). But this faith, this consuming desire for the real, is linked to a long-held political sentiment: the desire for class equality, the end of "aristocratic" dominance. After "long constraint in the respectable and money-making dens of existence," a man emerges to glimpse "the eternal," the "realities of things" (1:169, 170).[2] According to Whitman's Locofoco romanticism, to thus emerge would be to occupy not just a world of cleansed perception but, *a fortiori*, a more equal society.

But the paradox is that the speaker of "Song of Myself" almost immediately returns to the language of high culture to continue his metaphysical musings. "I have heard what the talkers were talking," he tells us, "the talk of the beginning or the end. But I do not talk of the beginning or the end" (*LG* 26). He continues, as if paraphrasing the talk he has overheard:

Urge and urge and urge,
Always the procreant urge of the world.

Out of the dimness opposite equals advance . . . . Always substance and
increase,
Always a knit of identity . . . . always distinction . . . . always a breed of
life. (26–27)

This is the metaphysical talk of the Concord transcendentalists, who had
begun to import German idealist philosophy into America. Whitman gets
his introduction to the subject from a book by one of the Concord circle,
Frederic Henry Hedge's *Prose Writers of Germany* (1848), which assembled
extracts from Hegel, Schelling, Fichte, Lavater, and Herder, among others.[3]
In his summary of Hegel's system, Hedge writes,

> There is one *Absolute Substance* pervading all things. That Substance is
> *Spirit*. This Spirit is endued with the power of development; it produces
> from itself the opposing powers of the universe. All that we have to do is
> stand by and see the process going on. The process is at first the evolution
> of antagonistic forces; then a mediation between them . . . which pro-
> duces a higher unity. This again is but the starting point for a new series.
> And so the process goes on.[4]

Whitman helps himself to "substance" and rewrites "opposing powers" as
"opposite equals," while putting Hegelian dialectics into the unfamiliar
context of sexual reproduction, the "procreant urge of the world." Whitman takes this latter notion from Schelling's "On the Relation of the Plastic Arts to Nature," which describes how nature appears to the "inspired
seeker" as "the holy, ever-creative original energy of the world, which gen-
erates and busily evolves all things out of itself."[5] He adds another term
from Hedge's introduction to Schelling, who "holds that matter and spirit,
the ideal and the real, subject and object, are identical. The Absolute,
according to him, is neither real nor ideal, (neither matter nor spirit,) but
the identity of both."[6] This idea Whitman glosses with the figurative "knit
of identity." Whitman seems to have acquired the last term in the sequence
from Schelling's essay, which argues that "no particular exists by means of
its limitation, but through the indwelling force with which it maintains
itself as a particular Whole, in *distinction* from the Universe."[7] Substance
and increase are realities Whitman validates for himself by appropriating

the language of idealist philosophy. "Song of Myself" begins, paradoxically, with parody, originally a song "sung in imitation of another."[8]

As Margaret A. Rose notes, parody involves "both nearness and opposition," consonance and transgression.[9] The first sign of opposition comes with the impatient, even testy, "To elaborate is no avail . . . . Learned and unlearned feel that it is so" (*LG* 27). The line signals a reluctance to follow all the permutations of spirit traced by Hegel and Schelling: a tension has been created by Whitman's careful treading of the border between nearness and opposition, imitation and critique. Parody involves ambivalence, since the parodist must to some extent know, love, and revere what he imitates for the imitation to be successful. At the same time, the parodist might also wish to mock, deface, or otherwise protest the imposing aspect of the object imitated, so intimidating in its authority, its inherited weight of tradition, or else its display of technical skill. By declaring that to elaborate is no avail, Whitman is going it alone, although (again ironically) he does so under license from another of Hedge's idealists, Fichte:

> I have hitherto relied on the care and fidelity of strangers in regard to the most important. I have imputed to others an interest in the highest concerns of Humanity, an earnestness, a precision which I had by no means discovered in myself. I have estimated them unspeakably higher than myself.
>
> Whatever truth they know, from whence can they know it except from their own reflection? And why may not I discover the same truth by the same reflection, since I avail as much as they? How have I hitherto undervalued and despised myself![10]

Fichte resolves not to heed others any longer: "I will investigate for myself . . . with severe accuracy I will go to work. With candor I will confess to myself the whole."[11] Thus instructed, Whitman can with confidence begin his song of himself with an emboldened, capitalized "I."

But things are getting too highfalutin. The introduction of "unlearned" marks the first stage of a descent from the lofty and the speculative to the low and the concrete. There is a sudden switch into the vernacular, or rather into jargon, the specialized language of one of Whitman's trades, as he prepares to discuss the mysterious unity of body and soul:

Sure as the most certain sure . . . . plumb in the uprights, well entretied,
  braced in the beams,
Stout as a horse, affectionate, haughty, electrical,
I and this mystery here we stand. (*LG* 27)

With *plumb* (vertical) and *entretied* (cross-braced), Whitman breaks into the language of carpentry as a seriocomic antidote to metaphysics. This is the variety of parody known as travesty, "the low burlesque of a particular work achieved by treating the subject of that work in an aggressively familiar style."[12] The contents of *Prose Writers of Germany* are brought down to the level of a Brooklyn house builder, circa 1855. The point of the travesty is relatively clear: meaning is better got at through a language close to the purposive activity of ordinary people than through the abstruse vocabulary of professional "talkers." Whitman travesties metaphysics by changing its clothes (to develop the metaphor concealed in the word's etymology); lapsing into carpenter-speak is part of the process of becoming undisguised and naked:

Knowing the perfect fitness and equanimity of things, while they
  discuss I am silent, and go bathe and admire myself. (27)

Whitman "knows" instinctively and through practice what the idealist knows in theory: that, in Lavater's words, "Man . . . is in himself the most worthy subject of observation, as he likewise is himself the most worthy observer. . . . He exists and moves in the body he inhabits, as in his element. This material man must become the subject of observation."[13] Furthermore, "Every thing in man is progressive, every thing congenial: form, stature, complexion, hair, skin, veins, nerves, bones, voice, walk, manner, style, passion, love, hatred. One and the same spirit is manifest in all."[14]

Whitman's calculated affront to decorum and good taste through the introduction of the incongruous and inappropriate—his breaking off to take a bath—is the first sounding of the satirical voice in "Song of Myself." Because we are not used to thinking of Whitman as a satirist, an excursus into the form is necessary. Whitman followed the example of a particular kind of satire, which embeds itself in the texture of the writing rather than announcing its intentions. The example, which contains its own ambiguities, was provided by Thomas Carlyle.[15]

Carlyle's *Sartor Resartus*, first published in Boston in 1836, purports to be the edited manuscripts of a German professor, Diogenes Teufelsdröckh, whose life's work is dedicated to a formal disquisition on the subject of clothes, although this is really an elaborate metaphysical allegory concerning the problem of distinguishing appearance and reality.

> Of good society Teufelsdröckh appears to have seen little, or has mostly forgotten what he saw. He speaks out with a strange plainness; calls many things by their mere dictionary names. To him the Upholsterer is no Pontiff, neither is any Drawing-room a Temple, were it never so begilt and overhung: "a whole immensity of Brussels carpets, and pier-glasses, an ormolu," as he himself expresses it, "cannot hide from me that such a Drawing-room is simply a section of Infinite Space, where so many God-created Souls do for the time meet together." To Teufelsdröckh the highest Duchess is respectable, is venerable; but nowise for her pearl-bracelets, and Malines laces: in his eyes, the star of a Lord is little less and little more than the broad button of a Birmingham spelter in a Clown's smock; "each is an implement," he says, "in its kind; a tag for *hooking-together*; and, for the rest, was dug from the earth, and hammered on a stithy before smiths' fingers." Thus does the Professor look in men's faces with a strange impartiality, a strange scientific freedom . . . "within the most starched cravat there passes a windpipe and wesand, and under the thickliest embroidered waistcoat beats a heart."[16]

Teufelsdröckh's "plainness" involves a stark, Anglo-Saxon vocabulary—broad button, spelter, smock, tag, hooking-together, dug, earth—which is combined with a philosophical vocabulary of sections and infinite space and flung aggressively at a language of early Victorian stuffiness and distinction: ormolu, respectable, venerable, implement, cravat. This is, in the words of the Editor, "a rich, idiomatic diction," where "picturesque allusions," alternate with "quaint tricksy turns" in "beautiful vicissitude."[17] But what is significant about Carlyle's style is that the barriers erected between the polite and the vernacular by the neoclassical standard—and maintained by southwestern humor—have been broken down, giving way to a promiscuous intermixing of languages, together with a tendency toward unrestrained coinage and innovation. Carlyle saw himself as part of a contemporary "revolution" marked by Sir Walter Scott's "Novel Scotch[,] . . . Irish, German, French, and even Newspaper Cockney," an ingress of dialect that meant that "the whole structure of our Johnsonian English" was "breaking up from its foundations."[18]

In shaping his own mixed style, Carlyle was directly influenced by the German novelist Jean Paul Richter, two of whose works, *Army-Chaplain Schmelzle's Journey to Flaetz* and the *Life of Quintus Fixlein*, he translated in 1827. Carlyle also singles out Lawrence Sterne as "our finest, if not our strongest . . . specimen of humour."[19] But both of Carlyle's stylistic sources draw in turn on the tradition of Menippean satire. The tradition comes down to us via the work of the Renaissance humanists and through the translations of Lucian by Erasmus and Sir Thomas More.[20] The principle of Menippean satire is the "shocking juxtaposition of irreconcilable opposites"; its verbal texture is made up of "recherche vocabulary, polyglot invention, combination of archaism and neologisms, variation in style and tone, and sheer delight in language."[21] Menippean satire reminds us that the term "satire" derives from the Latin *satur*, meaning "full." The Roman literary form, *satura*, meant a medley of outspoken comment on diverse subjects in a miscellany of forms; figuratively, satire presents a "platter of mixed offerings," a hotchpotch, gallimaufry, or olla podrida; *satura* is described by classical authorities as *miscillo* or *aggerans* (it is also *farcinat*, a kind of stuffing).[22]

An example of Menippean satire that discloses the genre's potential for political critique is provided by Lucian, a lowborn Syrian of the second century A.D., who perfected the technique of seriocomic "style-mingling." As the Greek ruling class settled into "comfortable acquiescence in Roman rule," they were constantly reminded of a basic incongruity, a "gap between the lackluster present and that exalted world . . . familiar from the literature of the classical and archaic periods."[23] In order to point out the existence of this gap, Lucian appealed to Menippus himself. In the *Double Indictment*, Dialogue describes how Zeus dragged him down from the "celestial vault" of philosophy and put me on the level of the average man. He took away my sober tragic mask, and gave me another, a mask for comedy and farce, that is all but absurd. Then he shut me up with Epigram and Lampoon and Cynicism and Eupolis and Aristophanes, great men for making fun of all that is sacred and ridiculing all that is right. Finally he even dug up Menippus, one of the old Cynics, whose bark is bad and whose bite is worse. . . . He smiles as he sinks his teeth in.[24]

Menippus was a Phoenician of servile origin, who lived in the third century B.C. Described as "a lone wolf on the fringes of the Cynic movement," he went about pretending to be an emissary from Hades, "sent to report on human sins," a man notorious for his mockery of all claims to truth and virtue, "Menippus the bogeyman."[25] In *Necyomantia* ("The Consultation of the Dead"), Lucian brings Menippus onstage as the "ludicrous cynic," dressed in Odysseus's felt cap, carrying Orpheus's lyre, and wearing Heracles' lion's skin, speaking in tags of Euripidean verse:

All hail, my roof, my doors, my hearth and home
How sweet again to see the light and thee!

Menippus then asks his friend Philonides what is going on in Athens. He replies, "Oh, nothing new; extortion, perjury, forty per cent., face-grinding."[26] Philonides punctures Menippus's elevated, classical rhetoric with a reminder of grimy contemporary realities, delivered in appropriately vulgar terms. Menippean satire exploits linguistic mixture for the purposes of social criticism, bringing down the lofty and elevating the low; it is also a sometimes veiled critique, smiling even as it sinks its teeth in.

Whitman absorbs the Menippean tradition through his reading of Carlyle, whose radically heterogeneous and satirically barbed style began to appeal to him just as he was about to hurl himself at the slavocracy, the ruling class of his own time and place. In October 1846 Whitman reviewed Carlyle's *On Heroes, Hero-Worship, and the Heroic in History*, recently published in Wiley & Putnam's Library of Choice Reading, noting that "[u]nder his rapt, weird, (grotesque?) style the writer of this work has placed—we may almost say *hidden*—many noble thoughts." He followed this with the wholly conventional, Augustan assertion that "[n]o great writer achieves anything worthy of him, by merely inventing a new *style*. Style in writing, is much as dress in society; sensible people will conform to the prevalent mode" (*J2* 89). By April of the following year, in a review of *Past and Present*, he had softened his criticism: "[o]ne likes Mr. Carlyle, the more he communes with him; there is a sort of fascination about the man. His weird wild way—his phrases, welded together as it were, with strange twist-ings of the terminatives of words—his startling suggestions—his taking up, fish-hook like, certain matters of abuse—make an *original* kind of composi-tion, that gets, after a little usage, to be strangely agreeable!" (244).[27] What made Carlyle's mixed style agreeable was that its confrontation of literary and vernacular languages provided Whitman with a way to discharge the social tensions between the mercantile elite and the "grand body of white workingmen" produced by the controversy over slavery. In "Song of Myself," Whitman uses a seriocomic style to lampoon the literary-mercantile elite and to carve out a lower-middle-class space for cultural assimilation, grab-bing hold of the elite's cultural goods even as he challenges the legitimacy of their power. The opposing tendencies toward political satire and cultural cel-ebration that produce Whitman's forked tongue derive from the uniquely fraught, Janus-faced situation of the late 1840s—that historical moment when America seemed at once ready to come together into some new, cosmi-cally ordained order and prepared to dash itself to pieces.

Whitman's Brooklyn carpenter who disputes with genteel metaphysi-cians is fully in the tradition of Yankee humor as summarized by Lawrence Buell, its language of "laconic stolidity" used to deliver "wry rebukes to the 'civilized.'"[28] But what I want to draw attention to is the aggression moti-vating the travesty: the Menippean snarl, the flash of the cynic's teeth. The carpentry and metaphysics passage of "Song of Myself" sets up a pattern that is repeated across the poem. First of all, the clash of linguistic registers produces a conflict that is social and economic in its basis: the educated elite have the leisure and the equipment to talk metaphysics, which the autodi-dact speaker lacks. By adopting their language he claims an equal right to join in the conversation of culture, although it is clear from his rather hur-ried and derivative improvisation that he has come rather late to the con-versation.[29] But the snarl is accompanied by a smile: having declared that to elaborate is no avail, the speaker assures us, "[l]earned and unlearned feel that it is so" (*LG* 27). Where there is "distinction" in the sense of difference, there is also "identity" in the sense of sameness: social opposites advance as equals and are united or "knit" together in a common knowledge, just as atoms behave democratically. "You shall listen to all sides and filter them from yourself," the speaker tells us (26). The filtering reduces the tension created by the disruption of the lexis, dissolving conflict in the open, pluralistic space of the poem. But conflict cannot be kept out of "Song of Myself." A flavor of contemporaneity, produced by the celebrated catalogs of the urban scene, spurs Whitman's Menippean impulse to lift the lid on the miseries and mysteries of antebellum New York.

A "lonesome" upper-class woman, "handsome and richly drest," watches from behind the blinds of her window, as "[t]wenty-eight young men bathe by the shore." "Where are you off to, lady?" Whitman asks, as she joins them in fantasy. "I see you, / You splash in the water there, yet stay stock still in your room." The beards of the men glisten "with wet," the choice of word marking the explicit sexualization of the passage; "[l]ittle streams" pass "all over their bodies" (*LG* 34). In fantasy, "tremblingly," the woman "seizes fast to them" and masturbates:

> They do not know who puffs and declines with pendant and bending
>   arch,
> They do not think whom they souse with spray. (34)

Entangled in the eroticism are elements of both sympathy and satire. To disentangle them, it's necessary to turn to Whitman's likely source, *Venus in Boston: A Romance of City Life* (1849) by the urban sensationalist and radical republican George Thompson. The novel opens with the narrator promising to "draw the curtain" and reveal "the secret history of things hidden from the public gaze."[30] This secret history includes that of Lady Adelaide Hawley, who complains,

> Oh . . . how terrible it is for a young and passionate woman to be linked in marriage to an old, impotent, cold, passionless being, who claims the name of man, but is not entitled to it! . . . Like the thirsty traveller in a barren waste, her soul yearns for an ocean of delights and pants and longs

in vain. . . . [T]is slavery, tis madness, to be chained for life to but one source of love, when a thousand streams would not satiate or overflow.[31]

The similarities between this speech and the scene of the twenty-eight bathers are striking: in both texts, the frustrated sexual desires of an isolated, patrician woman are imagined as a boundless, uncontainable flow. Whitman transforms the ocean of delights and the thousand streams into a single stream, filled with a mockingly precise number of male bodies. While Lady Hawley "pants and longs in vain," the woman at the window "puffs." Whitman keeps and elaborates on the autoeroticism of labored breath.[32]

In Thompson's novel, the Duchess, a confidence trickster, voices what can be taken as an item of Thompson's republican faith: the notion that "we all have derived from nature the right to feed our diversified passions according to their several cravings."[33] There are two problems, however. First of all, "a perverted and ridiculous PUBLIC OPINION prohibits such indulgences."[34] Second, class domination is reflected in sexual predation: the "lusts" of a class of "wealthy beasts" are allowed to "run riot on the innocence of young [working-class] females."[35] This situation means that, in the novel, gentlemen practice seduction while ladies are forced to compensate for this by preserving their "reputation and position."[36] The call for sexual equality—strident in the novel, muted in the poem—is vitiated somewhat by a certain ironic enjoyment of the upper-class woman's frustration: "Where are you off to, lady?" Whitman asks, a hint of plebeian mockery entering his voice.

So much for the sympathy, hedged about as it is by taunts. The satire is less easily located but works at a lower, more insistent pitch. David Reynolds argues that, with the twenty-eight bathers, "Whitman adopts the voyeuristic eroticism of the popular sensationalists but revises it in ways that make it natural and redemptive rather than selfish or destructive."[37] Whitman provides us with "refreshing, baptismal images," and with this "cleansing rhetoric" he "weds the sexual act with innocent frolic in nature."[38] I think that this is to sentimentalize the redemptive power of a putatively "high" literature, set in opposition to the degraded popular medium of sensationalism. The same prurience and the same class animus seem to me to adhere in Whitman's voyeurism and in Thompson's. The satire works through two elements: parataxis and diction.

The first element involves the structuring principle of the poem, the sequencing of its separate parts. The upper-class woman reaches climax, and in the next moment of paratactic simultaneity, we switch abruptly back to the speaker in the midst of a Bowery street scene:

> The butcher-boy puts off his killing-clothes, or sharpens his knife at the
>   stall in the market,
> I loiter enjoying his repartee and his shuffle and breakdown. (*LG* 34)

We move from patrician sterility to the vitality of white artisanal labor, so freely expressive in its physicality it can readily adopt the bodily *hexis* of the black strata beneath it.

Whites had become gradually more absorbed in black performance. African Americans in early eighteenth-century Manhattan gathered at Catherine Market. After selling their masters' produce, they would be "lured by some joking butcher or individual to engage in a jig or break-down."[39] They "tied their hair in tea-lead, combed it out to imitate the long wigs then in fashion, or wound their foreheads in eelskins." Fascinated whites paid to "overlay this black cachet on their own identities."[40] What evolved, through both blackface minstrelsy and black performance, was "a blending of Irish and Afro-American dance," the jig and the shuffle.[41] The fascination of black dance was that it "seemed to emphasize those aspects of the body that Europeans preferred to repress or deny," with the "lower body, or pelvis, as the axis and originator of movement."[42] The ex-slave Solomon Northup, in *Twelve Years a Slave* (1853), makes Whitman's satiric point more explicitly:

> Oh, ye pleasure-seeking sons and daughters of idleness, who move with measured step, listless and snail-like, through the slow-winding cotillon, if ye wish to look upon the celerity, if not the "poetry of motion"—upon genuine happiness, rampant and unrestrained—go down to Louisiana and see the slaves dancing in the starlight of a Christmas night.[43]

Black charisma was borrowed by white artisans. In April 1848 at the Chatham Theatre, Frank Chanfrau opened *New York As It Is*, the sequel to *A Glance at New York*. The play featured a black character, Porgy Joe, dancing for eels at Catherine Market; the playbill, promising a "NEGRO BREAK-

DOWN," displayed a lithographed image showing Chanfrau as Mose in full Bowery b'hoy regalia, admiring the blacked-up actor's flying feet.[44] A variant of the image shows a group of "stolidly middle-aged and middle-class men" watching the dancer from the edge of the picture, emphasizing both their "social distance" from the "loose and nimble motion" and the quiet absorption of Mose's gaze.[45] Whitman watches a butcher imitating the black dance imitated on the stage, as if hoping to acquire, even at one or two removes, the power summoned in his 1854 notebook: the power of "slipping like an eel through all blandishments and graspings." Whitman's calculated juxtaposition of leisure-class repression and artisanal spontaneity thrusts a satiric jab at Upper Tendom and begins a chain of "radical-democratic" reference points that stubbornly reiterate the charges of class division, inequality, and hypocrisy leveled at modern urban society by sensationalists like Thompson.

The satire extends to the diction of "Song of Myself" or, rather, buries itself in it. Whitman "loiters" by the butcher-boy's shop, enjoying his "repartee"; he watches the "grimed and hairy chests" of blacksmiths as they "environ the anvil" (LG 34, 35). Like elaborating to no avail, environing the anvil is comically excessive Latinity, a mock-heroic inflation of a mundane task, made starker by the proximity of the lowly "grimed" and "hairy." Similarly, the patrician woman "puffs," even as she "declines with pendant and bending arch," in another incongruous mix of diction. To "puff" is earthy, thirteenth-century Middle English (the *Oxford English Dictionary* gives a citation from *Piers Plowman*), while the Latinity of "decline" is exacerbated by its inclusion in a mock-Augustan periphrasis, an extremely roundabout way of putting things. A process of mutual interference between high and low registers is going on here. The hubristic pretension of the higher orders must be immediately punctured by low or vulgar expression, while the mundane activity of the lower orders is raised to a heroic level by the learned, Latinate word. This is Locofoco poetics, the work of the "democratic writer" described in Whitman's 1842 article on "Boz and Democracy." Whitman argues here that the business of the democratic writer is to "destroy those landmarks which pride and fashion have set up," to make us admit that "although social distinctions place others far higher or far lower than we, yet we are human beings alike, as links of the same chain; one whose lines are imbued, from preface to finis, with that philosophy which teaches to pull down the high and bring up the low" (*J1* 36). By switching between language levels, alternately deflating elite pretensions and elevating artisanal praxis, Whitman pursues the radical-democratic class struggle in language.[46]

After the Menippean snarl comes the "democratic" smile. Whitman goes on to make his claim to the democratic inclusiveness of the America for which he speaks:

> I am of old and young, of the foolish as much as the wise,
> Regardless of others, ever regardful of others,
> Maternal as well as paternal, a child as well as a man,
> Stuffed with the stuff that is coarse, and stuffed with the stuff that is
>   fine,
> One of the great nations, the nation of many nations—the smallest the
>   same and the largest the same,
> A southerner soon as a northerner, a planter nonchalant and hospitable,
> A Yankee bound my own way . . . . ready for trade [. . .] . (*LG* 40)

This could be easily dismissed as modish, Young America propaganda. But the claims are extraordinary nevertheless. It's hard not to balk at the reference to the planter, "nonchalant and hospitable," given Whitman's Free-Soil past. But the claims are, nevertheless, advanced seriously and underpinned by a concept of American democracy as a cosmic order, a complex, naturally evolving system:

> I resist anything better than my own diversity,
> And breathe the air and leave plenty after me,
> And am not stuck up, and am in my place.
>
> The moth and the fisheggs are in their place,
> The suns I see and the suns I cannot see are in their place,
> The palpable is in its place and the impalpable is in its place. (41)

"Diversity" has a particular, ideological resonance here. Whitman sings the song of himself as the song of the American cosmos, isolate self merging seamlessly into all-encompassing order of things—from the tiniest specks of matter to the almost unimaginably large stretches of the universe. In doing so, he participates in a midcentury ritual of consensus, one means by which a "stratified, conflicted society, rife with ethnic and class divisions," was able to become unified in its very diversity.[47] In this ritual, nature functions as the symbol of an organic whole that resolves its separate parts, producing a vision of an expanding nation in an expanding universe. The "infinite variety of nature"—her "interminable diversity"—provides a writer in the *Democratic Review* with the emblem for a capitalist democracy: "from the blade of grass which we crush beneath our feet, to the towering forests which spread continuous shade over half a continent; from the smallest grain of sand which sparkles on the sea-shore, to those magnificent worlds which lie sprinkled through the fields of space."[48] Just as nature allows infinite diversity among its constituent parts, differences between individuals in American society can attain "harmony" and "equilibrium."[49] This harmony is made possible by a "laissez-faire polity."[50] Its citizens join together long enough to "simplify government" and guarantee "universal equity," in the process giving "unbounded freedom to trade."[51] The symbol of America as "nature's nation" dissolves the threat of conflict: young and old, foolish and wise, southerner and northerner, planter and Yankee, are preserved in their nonantagonistic difference, held in the same relationship of "connection, resemblance, and order," as moth, fish eggs, and suns.[52]

But, in "Song of Myself," this ritual of consensus is not allowed to proceed smoothly or without interruption. Just when we have arrived at a vision of the ideal America, seen from the cosmic perspective of evolutionary time, the class invective of antebellum New York returns in a descent from Manifest Destiny to manifest inequality. Whitman pauses to consider "What is a man anyhow? What am I? and what are you?" It quickly becomes clear these are not questions to be answered in the register of the abstract or the ideal:

> I do not snivel that snivel the world over,
> That months are vacuums and the ground but wallow and filth,
> That life is a suck and a sell, and nothing remains at the end but
>   threadbare crape and tears. (*LG* 43)

Whitman refuses to join the embittered and nihilistic at the bottom of the pile. To indicate that he is referring to the lower orders, he includes, along with "wallow" and "filth," a sample of the slang that might be heard there: a "suck" is, according to Bartlett, "[a] cheat" or "deception." But Whitman also refuses the Latinate blandishments of genteel culture, whether religious or professional:

> Shall I pray? Shall I venerate and be ceremonious?
> I have pried through the strata and analyzed to a hair,
> And counselled with doctors and calculated close and found no sweeter
>   fat than sticks to my own bones. (43)

The sudden declension from "venerate," "ceremonious," "strata," and "analyzed" to the Anglo-Saxon solidities of fat sticking to bones marks another pointed turning away from refined talk. Whitman has selected what might be termed a middle register between Latinity and slang, an Anglo-Saxon "purity" capable of rebuffing both elite pretension and underclass whimpering with the simple, modest assertions of a lower-middle-class man. Whitman is not "stuck up," but neither is he a sniveler; he is in his cosmically appointed place, the place of the middle ground.

Place was necessarily a topic of prime concern in an antebellum New York "polarized between the opulent rich and the degraded poor."[53] With the homes of the gentry as yet confined to the area around lower Broadway, the mercantile elite and the plebeian horde lived in adjacent streets. In January 1847, Philip Hone observed that "[t]he two extremes of costly luxury in living, expensive establishments and improvident waste are presented in daily and hourly contrast with squalid mixing and hopeless destitution."[54] A new genre of what Stuart Blumin terms "nonfictional urban sensationalism" organized the New York of the 1840s around a series of "symbolic zones."[55] These zones extended from the "palaces and temples" of Broadway to the "squalid cellars" and "filthy holes" of Chatham Street and the Bowery.[56] Writers like George Foster located the pretension and depravity of the elite alongside the degradation and vice of the poor to construct a "moral geography" of the city.[57] The fundamental, republican premise of this geography is that polar opposites are joined in infamy: in five to ten years "all the gay and thoughtless creatures" of the "fashionable assignation-house" will be "drunkards in the kennels of the Five Points, full of loathsome diseases."[58] Foster's urban sensationalism is part of what Peter G. Buckley refers to as the struggle by the middle classes to fix the boundaries of a "virtuous middle ground," a "variable, shifting" space somewhere between opulence and degradation.[59]

In New York, a linguistic dimension to this struggle over cultural ground emerged in the literary-political battles between the genteel *Knickerbocker* set and the rising professionals of Young America. In a wider context, the antebellum period witnessed a range of linguistic clashes, with "gentry usage" colliding with "rude speech" to create what Kenneth Cmiel calls "middling styles," idioms that "easily mixed the refined and the raw."[60] The result, according to Cmiel, was that genteel norms were diffused alongside vernacular styles: in political oratory, popular preaching, and the penny press, the earthy was joined with the abstract, vulgarity with bombast. Cmiel argues that the middling style eroded class distinctions: "[t]he stylistic bricolage made it maddeningly hard to divide the world into the few and the many."[61] The "push" toward democratic rawness and the contrary "pull" toward genteel convention created "a kind of cultural vertigo," in which "[t]here was vulgarity among the few and refinements among the many."[62] This situation could also create "strange farragoes" within the speech of a single person, capable at any moment of being both folksy and erudite.[63] Antebellum America appears, in this account, as a carnivalesque culture, presided over by the lords of misrule.

I think that Cmiel's analysis contains a useful perception and a misrecognition. The useful perception is that of "cultural vertigo." Based on the evidence of "Song of Myself" and its sources, there was indeed a confusion and a mixing of cultural styles in the period, which tended to destabilize the speaking self. The misrecognition lies in the assumption of an exact homology between cultural forms and economic structure: if the boundaries between cultures are eroding, the argument goes, then it is because those between classes are eroding as well. But this is to "mistake the real and important margin of error in capitalist society for an overall loosening of class ties."[64] New York City in the 1840s witnessed no "easy" mixing of styles: the dominance of the literary-mercantile elite was too complete for that. Young America, certainly, found it hard to violate neoclassical decorum; the vernacular was safely quarantined in Yankee and southwestern humor, its sallies against the gentry carefully controlled and as likely to rebound on the backwoodsman as on the polite interlocutor. Whitman's political poetry of 1850 indicates how rigid the class lines still were and how difficult it was to mix languages, to break the carefully maintained borders between them.

That said, "vertigo" is a useful term to describe Whitman's predicament, for an ambiguity remains. Is the middling style to be used to Menippean effect, to attack the refined gentlemen who dabble here and there in vernacular earthiness, heedless of the material conditions of a life lived close to the ground? Or is the middling style a bid for mass audience approval, the solution to all contradictions, the cosmic-American order? Does "middling" suggest a principled rejection of social polarities or an attempt to cover all the bases? Even as one speaks, the middle ground begins to shift, inducing the vertigo of one who, in becoming elevated, is not sure whether his or her feet are still connected with anything more solid than speech. Witness the "strange farrago" within Whitman's declarations:

> And I know I am solid and sound,
> To me the converging objects of the universe perpetually flow,
> All are written to me, and I must get what the writing means. (*LG* 43)

The Anglo-Saxon simplicity of "solid" and "sound" gives way to the preciousness of converging objects perpetually flowing, a leap back into metaphysics from the sweet fat that sticks to the bones. The mixture amounts to a declaration of independence: Whitman claims to have located the Anglo-Saxon core of his social and linguistic being, but he is also, apparently, capable of engrafting Latinate high culture onto its sturdy stem. Philology acts as the antidote to cultural vertigo, a means of putting firm ground beneath one's feet.

Whitman sets out his language theory in the preface of *Leaves of Grass*:

> The English language befriends the grand American expression . . . it is brawny enough and limber and full enough. On the tough stock of a race who through all change of circumstances was never without the idea of political liberty, which is the animus of all liberty, it has attracted the

terms of daintier and gayer and subtler and more elegant tongues. [. . .] It is the chosen tongue to express growth faith self-esteem freedom justice equality friendliness amplitude prudence decision and courage. It is the medium that shall well nigh express the inexpressible. (*LG* 22–23)

From the evidence of this passage and the linguistic texture of "Song of Myself," it appears likely that Whitman had read Maximilian Schele De Vere's *Outlines of Comparative Philology* (1853) or, at least, absorbed its argument from another source.[65] De Vere describes how the "simple majesty of Saxon-English" was preserved under Norman political and linguistic oppression by "the humble and unlettered," along with its cognate virtues of "civil liberty" and "independence of faith"—values Whitman ascribes to the English language in the preface.[66] De Vere sets up a primary opposition between a Norman ruling class and a Saxon people, in which native words are overlaid with foreign ones: "[h]ills became *mountains* and dales *valleys*, streams were called *rivers*, and brooks *rivulets*, waterfalls changed into *cascades* and woods into *forests*."[67] Saxon resistance was concentrated in the language of the home: "there, around the *fireside* in his *kitchen* and the *hearth* in his *room*, [the Saxon] met his *beloved kindred*; the *bride*, the *wife*."[68] De Vere produces a narrative of "two languages, now contending and then mingling with each other"—a process that is repeated during the Renaissance period when "[t]he country was fairly overflooded with Latin."[69]

In the preface, Whitman equates Anglo-Saxon English with "liberty" and "faith," and he shares De Vere's hesitation over the extent to which languages contend or mingle. Saxon English, Whitman declares, is "the powerful language of resistance," the "dialect of common sense." In this sense, it is the enemy of the "swarms of the polished deprecating and reflectors and the polite"—the metaphysical talkers who do nothing but "reflect" abstrusely (*LG* 23). But this "brawny," abrasive English is also uniquely absorptive and adaptable, attracting the "terms of daintier and gayer and subtler and more elegant tongues," like French and Latin (22, 23). English is both the language of division and of mobility, of class contention and class mingling.[70]

The following verses of "Song of Myself" cement this understanding of English as a divided, composite language through a series of assertions in pointedly mixed diction:

I know I am august,
I do not trouble my spirit to vindicate itself or be understood,
I see that the elementary laws never apologize,
I reckon I behave no prouder than the level I plant my house by after all.
   (*LG* 44)

Whitman is "august," like an emperor, and his spirit needs neither to vindicate itself via Latinity nor to be understood in Anglo-Saxon—which is to say, it can express itself equally well in both. Whitman occupies a linguistic middle ground that implies a median class location: the shifting and variable space of the lower middle class. Moving into this space produces another revival of Whitman's artisanal jargon, intermixed with the highbrow philosophy of the autodidact:

My foothold is tenoned and mortised in granite,
I laugh at what you call dissolution,
And I know the amplitude of time. (44)

Whitman draws on and travesties another work of German idealism from Hedge's collection—this time Herder's "Metempsychosis, in Three Dialogues":

Do I know the world of lives which I call my body?. . . In my veins, in the minutest vascules alloted to me, these souls are pilgriming toward a higher life, as, already, through so manifold paths and preparations, they have travelled from all creation into me. I prepare them for their farther progress, as everything before has prepared them for me. No destruction, no death is there in creation, but *dissolution*, parturition, lustration.[71]

Once again, we are not allowed to forget that "Song of Myself" is a poem written by a Brooklyn carpenter and house builder who had been a respectable editor, an omnivorous digester of reprints, and visitor of libraries. He can laugh at what "you," the educated middle-class reader of Herder, call dissolution, while still embracing the promise of spiritual rebirth, the endless transmigration of souls. He knows the lingo and can use it along with his own, which is considerably more earthy and solid. While his soul lives in its current manifestation, it is securely fixed in its place with artisanal skill: tenoned and mortised in granite.

It's here, I think, that Whitman hits his stride as a poetic innovator, with a newly apparent confidence in his technique and purpose. We are presented with a kind of double-voiced utterance, which says the same things twice, in alternate registers. "Song of Myself" constantly offers us alternative locutions, a carefully prepared smorgasbord of mixed offerings (emphases are mine):

I chant a new chant of dilation *or* pride [. . .]. (*LG* 44)

We have had ducking *and* deprecating about enough. (45)

Extoller of amies *and* those that sleep in each others' arms. (46)

Walt Whitman, an American, one of the roughs, a kosmos. (48)

If America has evolved as a "natural," democratic cosmos, then the American language has evolved in similar fashion, creating a Hegelian synthesis of all the world's languages:

Endless unfolding of words of ages!
And mine a word of the modern . . . . a word en masse. (47)

What was a linguistic incongruity bearing the marks of class division becomes a conscious admixture, the guarantee of an apparently stable class location—the position of a speaker who can select his words from above and below and reach out confidently to those who will follow in his footsteps:

Eleves I salute you,
I see the approach of your numberless gangs [. . .]. (69)

The absorptive width of Whitman's linguistic embrace is based on his location and occupation of the middle ground.

So confident is Whitman now in handling his mixed diction, he can deploy it to describe perplexity and confusion and make sense of complexity by the technique of reducing it to the play of relatively simple opposites: "I hear the trained soprano . . . . she convulses me like the climax of my love-grip" (*LG* 52). The orgasmic convulsions induced by the soprano are translated from

Latinity into a Teutonic/Anglo-Saxon coinage, the kind of compounding Carlyle practices when he describes the viscera as "life-tackle."[72] The passage goes on to reproduce the pattern. The orchestra "wrenches unnamable ardors from my breast" in lofty, poetic fashion, then "throbs me to gulps of the farthest down horror," which is both earthy and catachrestic. The speaker continues with the same construction—"[i]t sails me . . . . I dab with bare feet"—then returns to the higher register: he is "[s]teeped amid honeyed morphine" like some romantic votary of sensation, while his "windpipe" is more vulgarly "squeezed in the fakes of death," a sudden switch to the language of seafaring with the word for the coils of a rope. Finally, he is

Let up again to feel the puzzle of puzzles,
And that we call Being. (52)

"We" call the puzzle "Being" now: metaphysicians and sailors share the same mixed discourse in a kind of parody of the seriocomic style of *Moby-Dick* (1851), where whale hunters hover over "Descartian vortices."[73] Whitman does the opera, as it were, in different voices, combining the languages of upper-class exquisite and lower-class rough, lately arrived from the docks.

————

But I've made all this sound too smoothly and easily accomplished. Signs of tension, conflict, and disturbance remain within the "democratic *mélange*" of voices. The disturbance concerns the echoes of violence awakened by plebeian voices at the opera. On August 4, 1847, Whitman saw a performance by Mrs. Anna Bishop in an English version of Donizetti's *Linda di Chamounix* at the Park Theater. He informed the readers of the *Eagle* that

[h]er voice is the purest soprano—and of as silvery clearness as ever came from the human throat—rich, but not massive—and of such flexibility that one is almost appaled [*sic*] at the way the most difficult passages are not only gone over with ease, but actually dallied with, and their difficulty redoubled. They put one in mind of the gyrations of a bird in the air. (*J2* 304)

Whitman's references to an appalling difficulty, a perilous stability, hard-won against buffeting currents, link the opera review and the poem. But the context of Whitman's admiration of an English soprano is one of increasingly sharpened opposition between the elite and the populace of Manhattan.

The 1846–47 theatrical season coincided with the campaign for cultural nationalism waged under the banner of Young America. Anglophobia had been stirred by the dispute over the Oregon territory, which for a moment threatened war with Great Britain. Joining in the rhetoric of this campaign, Whitman abused the performances of the English actress Ellen Tree and her husband, Charles Kean, the "tawdry glitter of foreign fame" threatening to displace "our own stock performers" (*J2* 44–45, 44). Like the "oyster-cellar litterateurs" who mocked Kean's mannerisms, Whitman preferred the robust, republican acting style of Edwin Forrest, the hero of the Bowery b'hoys.[74] Whitman sprang to the defense of Young America, supporting Cornelius Mathews's call for a copyright law to protect American writers. "Among the sights that go to make a man's stomach qualmy," he told the *Eagle*'s readers on January 12, 1847, "is that monkeyism of literature, involved in a few gentlemen . . . getting together and 'adoring' and 'doting' on Byron, Scott, and 'sentiment'" (166). The baiting of genteel English performers and writers was part of a literary-political controversy conducted within the more or less secure confines of the Manhattan press.

But the Bowery's "egalitarian robustness," its "truculent antiauthoritarianism" found expression in more physical abuse, involving the ritual pelting of "snobbish English actors."[75] That robustness was matched in the mid-1840s by a revival of working-class militancy: a resurgence of craft organizations, an outbreak of strikes in the trades, and the revolt in 1846 of the Irish laborers of the Brooklyn waterfront, who "asserted in sweeping republican prose their own 'immutable rights to self-government,' to protect their own 'freedom and equality.'"[76] Alongside these developments, the mid-1840s saw the rise of the "shirtless Democrats," an "unorthodox group of largely working-class partisans," led by the "radical Bowery B'hoy politician" Mike Walsh.[77] At the other end of the social scale, the hegemony of the more restrained Knickerbocker elite was broken by the conspicuous consumption of a "parvenu aristocracy" keen to flaunt its wealth and privilege.[78] From January 1845, the penny press made the antics of the "Upper Ten" an object of ridicule after their chronicler, Nathaniel Parton Willis, proposed turning Broadway into a fashionable carriage drive.[79] The Upper

Ten were rechristened the "codfish aristocracy" by popular newspapers like James Gordon Bennett's *Herald*, by the Democratic press, and by nativist papers like E. Z. C. Judson's *Ned Buntline's Own*.

Whitman joined this ritual abuse of the city's elite. On March 28, 1846, he declared in the *Eagle* that "[n]ine out of ten of that perfumed, finical, dainty faction will not touch a sturdy workingman's hand, large and dark with honest labor" (*J1* 308). In the same month, Forrest hissed the "aristocratic" English actor Charles Macready during his performance of *Hamlet*. Then the *New York Herald* reported that Forrest had been humiliated by "illiberal and blackguard" British critics.[80] The stage was set for the open conflict that erupted at the Astor Place Opera House on May 10, 1849: Macready, pelted and driven from the stage by the b'hoys, only to return at the urging of "the respectable, literary and philosophical portion of the city";[81] the tragedian defended by a militia "officered and manned" by the derided class of "exclusives";[82] the "noise of the stones striking against the muskets," the "hallooing of the people";[83] the "guns, charged with grape, enfilad[ing] . . . the streets";[84] the eighteen who fell, the four more who died of their wounds.

Whitman, then, played a minor, incidental role in the chain of events leading to the Astor Place riot, the most dramatic example of class conflict in antebellum America: "the rich against the poor—the aristocracy against the people."[85] But the place and meaning of plebeian voices at the opera are already a live political issue by August 1847, when Whitman is so unsettled by the trained soprano. His discomfort and his mixed diction derive from his ambiguous class-cultural location, which is somewhere between Mike Walsh and N. P. Willis—the shirtless Democrat and the genteel journalist. While the b'hoys derided all pretensions to "culture," Whitman's lower-middle-class status and the social aspirations of his class meant he had to be more discriminating. He committed the *Eagle* on March 12, 1846 to the task of "[p]olishing the [c]ommon people." A sort of "democratical artistic atmosphere" might be "cheaply and conveniently" spread, Whitman thought, through "the more frequent diffusion of tasty prints, cheap casts of statuary, and so on" (*J1* 279). On November 21, Whitman told his readers that "we 'go' heartily for all the rational refinements and rose-colorings of life—such as music, mirth, works of art, genial kindness, and so forth. We wish every mechanic and laboring man and woman in Brooklyn, would have some such adornment to his or her abode—however humble that abode may be" (128). This artistic atmosphere couldn't afford to be too anglophobic. After all, the Harpers' sumptuous, illustrated edition of Milton, with its "thick white paper of superfine quality," its binding of "durable morocco," and its gilt ornaments "designed by the hand of taste," could only add distinction to its owners (395). Whitman also recommended the "gems from the rich treasury of instruction" contained in Charles Knight's *Half Hours with the Best Authors*, "within itself a complete course of general reading," with selections from Carlyle, Pascal, Bacon, Coleridge, and Hazlitt (336); the Harpers' *Memoirs of the Most Eminent American Mechanics*, a work lying "peculiarly within the province of good reading for the *young workingmen* of this republic" (180); and the fifth edition of *The American Poulterer's Companion*, "a practical treatise on the breeding, rearing, fattening, and general management of the various species of domestic poultry—with illustrations, and portraits of fowls 'taken from life'" (175). The review pages of the *Eagle* chart the shifting space of the "virtuous middle ground" and its "cultural vertigo": in them, as Joseph Rubin observes, "[l]ove of frontier and eagle alternat[e] with English meadow and nightingale," Kit Carson with Keats.[86]

While the literary-mercantile elite were distancing themselves from the "rowdiness" of the lower classes, Whitman remained committed to the "mingling" as well as the "contending" of classes because of the social and cultural benefits of such interaction to the self-improving citizen. In "A Visit to the Opera," an unpublished article describing the soprano Marieta Alboni, who performed in New York in the summer of 1852, Whitman recalled that "[a]ll persons appreciated Alboni—the common crowd quite as well as the connoisseurs. We used to go in the upper tiers of the theatre, (the Broadway,) on the nights of her performance, and remember seeing that part of the auditorium packed full of New York young men, mechanics, 'roughs,' & c., entirely oblivious of all except Alboni" (*NUPM* 1:396). The oblivion obtained by hearing the trained soprano though is vitiated by the vertigo it induces: the mixed accents of plebeian and aristocrat and the whiff of grapeshot the encounter portends. For what Whitman is describing in the "trained soprano" verse, after all, is the experience of *not* being securely in one's place but of being displaced—convulsed, wrenched, exposed, suffocated. The linguistic sea changes of Whitman's diction indicate that his social position is perhaps not after all as secure, as mortised and tenoned, as he has claimed: occupying the virtuous middle ground as "arbiter of the diverse" is as potentially anxious a position as plying one's trade in a turbulent market (*LG* 8).

The writer of "Song of Myself" was himself out of place. Whitman was, by the mid-1850s, more than ever an outsider: a newspaperman who had failed to progress in his career through devotion to political principle and through a lack of "polished" acquaintance. Joseph Rubin provides a vivid sketch of Whitman's marginal, dislocated state:

> He passed Bixby's, where sometimes he could see the ageing Cooper, Halleck, Whipple, and other literati, but he could not join them in the lobby or at Friday evening sessions of the Sketch Club; Anne Lynch did not invite editors of defunct papers or occasional columnists of the Sunday press to her salon at Waverly Place. Nor did Duyckinck have him in to eat brandied peaches side by side with Melville, Mathews, and Dana, and afterwards entrain with them for Olympian weekends in the Berkshires.[87]

Both *Knickerbocker* and Young American circles were composed of gentlemen and thus closed to Whitman the "shirt collar man," the itinerant editor who made a living in the exposed, indeterminate zone of the lower middle class. Whitman recalled for Horace Traubel how he had been "left out" of Duyckinck's *Cyclopedia of American Literature* and how he was not "accepted" in New York by "the great bogums," by "men of truly proper style" like Duyckinck.[88] For Whitman to flee the perfumed salon for the river bank is to reject a milieu that had already rejected him.

It is in order to banish such anxieties that Whitman plays up his role as mediator, occupying a space that defuses social tensions by turning them into opportunities for exchange. In 1852, George N. Sanders had penned an incendiary Young America editorial in the *Democratic Review* on the subject of "Fogy Literature," satirizing the "attenuated figure, dyspeptic system, shattered nerves, neuralgic stupidity, rheumatic inertness, agueish trepidation, chronic dishonesty, and feverish uncertainty" of the merchant-literary elite.[89] Whitman provides his own representative portrait in "Song of Myself":

You there, impotent, loose in the knees, open your scarfed chops till I
blow grit within you,
Spread your palms and lift the flaps of your pockets,
I am not to be denied . . . . I compel . . . . I have stores plenty and to
spare,
And any thing I have I bestow. (*LG* 70)

The scarfed chops are the silk-wrapped jowls of the effete upper-class gentleman, matched in sartorial splendor by his pocket flaps. Whitman offers to
revitalize him with an infusion of Anglo-Saxon vigor; "grit" is a pointedly
vulgar Americanism used by Davy Crockett to regale the polite circles of
Congress: "[h]onor and fame from no condition rise. It's the grit of a fellow
that makes the man."[90] But if he is capable of lobbing plebeian rebukes at
the overrefined, Whitman also makes it clear that he is prepared to absorb
the full range of elite cultural reference diffused by the antebellum culture of
reprinting:

Magnifying and applying come I,
Outbidding at the start the old cautious hucksters,
The most they offer for mankind and eternity less than a spirt of my
own seminal wet,
Taking myself the exact dimensions of Jehovah and laying them away,
Lithographing Kronos and Zeus his son, and Hercules his grandson,
Buying drafts of Osiris and Isis and Belus and Brahma and Adonai,
In my portfolio placing Manito loose, and Allah on a leaf, and the
crucifix engraved,
With Odin, and the hideous-faced Mexitli, and all idols and images,
Honestly taking them all for what they are worth, and not a cent
more [. . .]. (71–72)

Recent critics have taken Whitman at his word. Lawrence Buell presents
Whitman as going further than the "straitlaced" Emerson in the direction of
"Rabelaisian carnivalization."[91] Buell notes that Whitman replaces the "old-
fashioned, ponderous sermonic-scriptural language" with "hucksterese" but
at the same time retains "the older framework" so as to "give his advertise-
ments for himself solemnity and divine sanction, as well as the thrill of

irreverence."[92] In other words, Buell reads Whitman's linguistic strategy as entirely self-promoting and sensationalist, "a collage of the demotic and the high-falutin'" that "both jars and exhilarates."[93] Whitman, according to David Reynolds, "was able to bring democratic zest to elite images and philosophical depth to popular ones. The cross-fertilization of different images, he hoped, might help to disperse the various ills he and the nation faced."[94] What both Buell and Reynolds miss entirely is the political salience of Whitman's mixed style: all traces of class confrontation and tension are erased. Beneath the upbeat hucksterism, it's still possible, I think, to hear the Menippean snarl.

The point about Whitman's "carnivalesque" appropriations of high culture and his apparently neutral arbitration of the refined and the coarse is that he is, in fact, far from neutral: he takes up the definite position of his class, albeit on shaky ground. In another sudden change of tack, Whitman declares that he is able to discover "as much or more" in "a framer framing a house" than in the combined religious wisdom of East and West, of such absorbing interest in Concord: "[p]utting higher claims for him there with his rolled-up sleeves, driving the mallet and chisel." The people he says he values are "[t]hose ahold of fire-engines"; "the mechanic's wife with her babe at her nipple"; "three lusty angels," scything at harvest; and "the snag-toothed hostler" who sells all he possesses and travels on foot, in order "to fee lawyers for his brother and sit by him while he is tried for forgery" (*LG* 72). Whitman now speaks, not on behalf of American "diversity," but for workers in the city and in the fields who suffer at the hands of predatory lawyers and of capital owners:

> Tickets buying or taking or selling, but in to the feast never once going;
> Many sweating and ploughing and thrashing, and then the chaff for
>   payment receiving,
> A few idly owning, and they the wheat continually claiming. (73)

"A few idly owning" is a revival of radical, Locofoco sentiment from the 1840s and must have been inspired by the political and economic conditions in which Whitman completed his poem.

In the winter of 1851 the banks collapsed, and there followed "a veritable carnival of beggary by the unemployed."[95] In the winter of 1852 the journeymen carpenters were on strike for seventeen shillings a day. In the spring, Whitman set up as a builder and seller of small houses—a period of prosperity swiftly ended by the depression of the following spring, when banks and businesses once again failed and "gangs of destitute young girls, filthy and obscene" roamed the streets.[96] Unemployed in 1854, Whitman worked on his poems while mechanics marched with banners reading "if work be not given we will help ourselves to bread." On the other side of the social chasm, Mrs. William Colford Schermerhorn threw a lavish costume ball, the details available to the populace for a penny.[97] Whitman noticed the huge numbers of "wants" ads placed in the newspapers by job seekers and penned an article on the subject. "Those of our readers, in the country," he writes,

> who jog along their solid, easy way, and are not in danger of falling on slippery places, know very little of the shifts and frequent desperations of the existence of the poor in cities. . . . These "wants" in the news papers are illustrative of the precarious nature of employment and existence here.—The merchants and prosperous mechanics do not appear in their columns. (*NUPM* 1:88, 89)

No matter how hard Whitman tries to spiritualize and resolve social conflict by presenting himself as the arbiter of the diverse, the clashing linguistic registers of his poetry revive it. The filthy beggar girls are airbrushed from the picture of the metropolis in "Song of Myself," but the signs of class friction reemerge through the mixed diction, which doesn't so much dissolve social boundaries as highlight them.

It is at this point of radical-democratic sympathy that Whitman is prepared to take a rare—perhaps his only—glance down at the strata lying just beneath the lower middle class: a level to which that class might all too easily slip. Whitman states his belief in "what is untried and afterward" in the great shadow of American futurity:

> It cannot fail the young man who died and was buried,
> Nor the young woman who died and was put by his side,
> Nor the little child that peeped in at the door and then drew back and
> was never seen again,

Nor the old man who has lived without purpose, and feels it with
    bitterness worse than gall,
Nor him in the poorhouse tubercled by rum and the bad disorder,
Nor the numberless slaughtered and wrecked . . . . nor the brutish
    koboo, called the ordure of humanity,
Nor the sacs merely floating with open mouths for food to slip in,
Nor any thing in the earth, or down in the oldest graves of the earth,
Nor any thing in the myriads of spheres, nor one of the myriads of
    myriads that inhabit them,
Nor the present, nor the least wisp that is known. (*LG* 76)

True, this isn't a very edifying spectacle. There's possibly even less actual
human sympathy here than in the accounts of a series of polite visitors to
the Five Points, Manhattan's miasmic slum, notorious for the squalor of its
crammed tenements, its prostitution, its racial mixing, and its gang violence. Dickens, with his *American Notes* (1842), sets the tone for sensationalists and reformers alike, with a mixture of sympathy and disgust: "What
place is this, to which the squalid street conducts us? . . . What lies beyond
this tottering flight of steps, that creak beneath our tread?—a miserable
room, lighted by one dim candle, and destitute of all comfort. . . . Conceive
the fancies of a feverish brain, in such a place as this! . . . all that is loathsome, drooping, and decayed is here."[98] George Foster fills in some of the
details in *New York in Slices* (1849):

> "[A] few steps bring us to the great central ulcer of wretchedness—a very
> rotting skeleton of civilization, whence emanates an inexhaustible pesti-
> lence. . . . But let us enter one of these dark abodes . . . the bloated mis-
> tress of the house, [stands] ready to administer drugged brandy . . . [h]alf
> a dozen disgusting wretches who ought to be women, are lounging upon
> the benches in immodest attitudes. . . . A heap of rags . . . stirs in the cor-
> ner. . . . Even while we gaze, the jaw falls, and, with a gurgling impreca-
> tion, the spirit of the prostitute seeks its Maker.[99]

Solon Robinson provides another eyewitness account in *Hot Corn* (1854):

> The entrance is in Cow Bay. If you would like to see it, saturate your hand-
> kerchief with camphor, so that you can endure the horrid stench, and

enter. Grope your way through the long, dark, narrow passage—turn to your right, up the dark and dangerous stairway; be careful where you place your foot around the lower step, for it is more than shoe-mouth deep of steaming filth. . . . Look; here is a negro and his wife sitting upon the floor . . . eating their supper off the bottom of a pail . . . there is no bed in the room—no chair, no table—no nothing—but rags, and dirt, and vermin, and degraded, rum degraded, human beings.[100]

Destitution, wretchedness, disease; prostrate, enervated figures, barely human in their utter passivity, their lack of both physical definition and animate will—these essential tropes of the Five Points are caught up by Whitman and the picture reduced to its barest outlines. In "Song of Myself" there's no zesty reportage or sharp, visual detail to make this picture come alive. This is something like the zero degree of the democratic catalog: its vanishing point, the point at which sharply defined, self-reliant citizens become tenuous membranes with open mouths. Foster has a heap of rags, Robinson a bloated mistress of the house and a Negro and his wife, eating from the bottom of a pail. Whitman has "sacs merely floating," the Latinate word marking his distance from the spectacle, emptying it of all its human particularity.

Whitman's journalism is so typically concerned with "polishing the common people" that it rarely fixes its attention on the lower depths. Nevertheless, it's possible to detect in Whitman's editorials on urban problems a profound ambivalence. On the one hand, Whitman wants to redeem even the possibility of vice with both rigorous self-improvement and a concerted program of reform. The voice of Whitman the urban reformer is loud and clear: Brooklyn deserves to be christened "the city of dirt" (*J2* 272). Its streets and gutters are filled with "filth, mud, and street refuse," so that after heavy rain they become "little but a mass of mud and liquid nastiness" (273). Whitman campaigns in his editorials for both clean, well-lit streets and hygienic citizens, advertising the health-giving benefits of regular bathing: "put your carcasses under water everyday, and when you emerge, use the brush vigorously for five minutes. There is nothing like the pure bracing water" (313).

But when it comes to tackling more intransigent social problems—poverty, disease, vice—Whitman's voice is more restrained and conflicted.

Offering "A Few Words to the Young Men of Brooklyn," Whitman urges that "instead of spending so many hours, idling in bar-rooms, and places of vapid irrational un-amusement," these urban youths should "occupy their time in improving themselves in knowledge" (*J2* 151). It pains him to see "so many intelligent looking boys idling at the corners, or around certain classes of shops—gradually becoming tainted, and growing up as the weeds grow" (176) or to witness the children of the poor "beset on every side" with "danger—with poisonous habits, and wretched imitations" (116). Whitman the respectable Brooklyn editor is afflicted by a wholly conventional squeamishness, hobbling his own reforming impulse by a refusal to name the problem he seeks to remove. Polite circumlocutions—"certain classes of shops," "becoming tainted"—have to suffice instead of "grog shops," "drunkenness," and "the use of prostitutes." "Sacs merely floating" and "myriads of spheres" belong to a similar order of euphemism.

Whitman's laissez-faire faith frustrates and complicates his sympathies with the working people of his own city. Considering the issue of "Illy Paid Labor in Brooklyn," Whitman's sympathies are aroused by "the cause of the laborer, or a band of laborers, struggling for a competence" and "standing out against the exactions of grinding 'bosses' and speculators" (*J1* 303). But Whitman's unswerving commitment to the free-market principle means that he issues, in the next breath, a condemnation of "organized associations, to 'regulate' the prices of labor." Workers cannot be allowed to bargain collectively for higher wages: "trade and prices" must be left "to regulate themselves." Nevertheless, Whitman cannot escape the feeling that market forces, left to themselves, produce injustice. "We understand," he says, "that the sum which has been paid" for the Brooklyn workmen's labor "from sunrise until dark, is sixty-four and a half cents each." Moreover, "they are closely overlooked," and any man late for roll call by three minutes has a quarter of his "miserable stipend" deducted. And, Whitman continues, "many of these men have families of children to feed, and clothe, and *educate*—and potatoes are a dollar a bushel, and flour and beef unusually high!" (304). All Whitman can offer is a moral exhortation to employers to be more generous; although, of course, if employers were to pay above the market rate, this too would contradict the principle of unregulated exchange.

The contradictions of Whitman's position—forthright advocacy of untrammeled market forces together with genuine sympathy for the market's victims—are made plain by his response to the Brooklyn laborers' dispute. For these are the very men Whitman wants to see recruited to clean the city's streets and to address with their labor the problem of that "mass of mud and liquid nastiness"—the street cleaners of Brooklyn, who have decided to lay down their tools and strike against their employer for better wages. Whitman wants the "dirt heaps" taken away "rapidly," but the labor power performing the task must not organize itself or act collectively in defense of its individual members. "Oppress Not the Hireling!" Whitman thunders, after a delegation from the Laborer's Association visits his office to explain their action. He is, once again, moved by their plight and powerless to help. In the absence of a class politics capable of aiding the "many sweating" in their struggles against "the few idly owning," the Brooklyn laborers must make do with "the outpourings of honest heart-impulses" (*J1* 316). Meanwhile, the dirt heaps remain.

When he considers the exploitation of women workers, Whitman is just as contradictory. He is appalled at how many "poor young women" there are in Brooklyn and New York, "made so by the miserably low rate of wages paid for women's work, of all kinds," from that of "the most accomplished governess" to that of "the washerwoman." But Whitman's worries are less with the mechanism of exploitation and how that mechanism may be politically influenced than with the physical and moral effects of grindingly hard and poorly paid work on the female body. Such work "takes away the blood" from the workingwomen's cheeks, removes also "the lustre from their eyes and the vigor from their young limbs, making them prematurely old, and giving them a few dollars instead" (*J2* 177). It also leads directly to "female crime": "On one side is virtue, but accompanied by stern and gaunt attendants—wearying labor, stinted food, mean dress, and the cool regard of the world. On the other side is vice, but smiling and buxom—offering pleasure, and easy life, comfort, and fine apparel. Is not the temptation great?" (178). Whitman rests content, for the moment, with this representation of the economic forces driving the prevalence of prostitution. Political economy becomes a melodramatic battle over a young woman's soul, a battle that results in either female crime or an application at the office of the Superintendents of the Poor. "[R]educed from comfort to poverty," the woman of the working poor "fight[s] with effort and pride against the evil day" but is forced to seek charitable support. Whitman stations himself in the office and reports the spectacle:

> The misery of her heart is fearfully plain upon her pinched and pallid features. Her frame totters and sways—her limbs are shaken with the palsy of her condition—her tongue is frozen and soundless; and it is only when the weak blood concentrates in its last blush for shame, and warmth follows tears, that the poor one (God pity her!) is able to articulate. She has come to *beggary* at last. (179)

This local intelligence of the poor in Brooklyn conveys powerfully the fear of falling that motivates the strenuous pursuit of self-improvement and stimulates the lower-middle-class autodidact's thirst for knowledge. But self-improvement is all but useless as a remedy for life at the borders of destitution. Whitman, all too aware of the futility of offering cheap reprints to those who cannot afford to eat, falls silent on the issue of a solution. It will "somehow or other follow—for benevolence, when aroused among the body of the people, tends to the reform of whatever abuse it is directed against" (178).

A complex set of emotions, therefore, lies behind Whitman's representation of urban poverty in "Song of Myself." But the association of economic distress and dirt is the consistent thread linking his reportage. Both the fear of contamination and the need for repeated, ritual acts of cleansing extend into Whitman's commentary on the popular press. In a series of articles, Whitman lambasts a rival publication, the *Brooklyn Daily Advertiser*, a paper edited by what he refers to as a "nest of English cockneys" or "migrating gentry from the stews of English cities." These disreputable gentlemen seek to capture readers by offering up cheap sensationalism, "all that is low and morbid, that corrupts and violates the rules of taste" (*J2* 293). The paper is corrupted by its "low-bred vulgarity"; it aims only to "regal[e] the morbid appetite of the lowest-class of scandal-lovers" (299). Whitman's reaction is violent because the *Advertiser* threatens to wreck the project of "unlimited self-improvement," the program of "polishing the common people" that he has been pursuing with the *Eagle*. The lower middle class of Brooklyn and

New York, those "young men or boys nearly grown—clerks, apprentices, office-boys, and so on" hurrying along with "bright faces" and "exact attire" (63), are at risk of being dragged down to the lowest level, the level of "the gutter-dirt that is washed into the dock by a shower" (293).

The same violence, the same fear, prompts the horrified notation in "Song of Myself" of the "sacs merely floating with open mouths for food to slip in": the sight of a human degradation terrifying in its passivity, its utter dearth of moral or mental resource. But the autodidact's pride in his own contrasting improvement steals in amid the hopelessness and filth. Where Robinson has passageways deep in "steaming filth," Whitman refers to the "brutish koboo, called the ordure of humanity"—a reference he seems to have got from a book by the American adventurer Walter M. Gibson, *The Prison of Weltevreden; and a Glance at the East Indian Archipelago* (1855). Gibson's book describes a visit to "the country north of Palembang," on the island of Sumatra:

A great many extraordinary and improbable stories are told about the Kubus and other wild aboriginal races, by the Malays, who call them by the general name of orang utan. Some account of them was given by a lieutenant in the army of Netherland India, who spent many years in Sumatra. . . . He spoke of them as a race of beings, living in a state of nature, as simple as wild beasts. They were much stronger built than the civilized men of the island; symmetrically formed, of powerful frame, and capable of enduring any hardships incident to their brutish life.

It appears that Whitman stitched in the reference to the "brutish koboo" from his recent reading, very near to the point when he completed "Song of Myself," misspelling their name but borrowing Gibson's epithet for them.[101] Intrigued by the legends he has heard, Gibson ventures into the jungle in search of the Kubu and eventually discovers them: "These were the *tai orang*, the refuse of men. . . . They were brutes, they had no worship, no marriage, no law, no clothing, no idea of its use; they were the accursed of Allah, companions of djins on earth; fit only to be beasts of burden."[102] "Song of Myself" translates Gibson's "refuse of men" into "ordure of humanity," via Robinson's "steaming filth." The inhabitants of the Five Points join the Kubu in the place of "degradation" Whitman feared that free white labor would be condemned to by the spread of slavery, "sunk to the miserable level of what is little above brutishness" (*J2* 319). But anthropology furnishes useful knowledge, a way of lifting the self above the threatening mire of its contemporary surroundings, the perplexing social evils of antebellum New York. Seeing the urban poor as an obscure Malaysian tribe earns the autodidact a momentary glow of distinction, casting a ray of disinfecting sunlight into the confounding gloom.

Whitman continues with this strategy of incorporating his improving reading into reportage, mixing the lofty and the abstruse into the exigencies and urgencies of the present moment. He folds the sociological horror of the Five Points back into the cosmos or, even more vaguely, the shadow of futurity—into "what is untried and afterward," where all will be well (*LG* 76). In the midst of class division and social degradation, Whitman clings to the destinarian faith that "the order of nature is a foreshadowing of that which is to be."[103]

"It is time to explain myself," Whitman announces, although the explanation is, on the face of things, rather obscure, not to say bombastic: "I am an acme of things accomplished, and I an encloser of things to be" (*LG* 77). Whitman declares that he is able to see into "the huge first Nothing," that he "waited unseen" in the "lethargic mist" at some point before the creation of the world. The language becomes increasingly dense and recondite:

My embryo has never been torpid . . . . nothing could overlay it;
For it the nebula cohered to an orb . . . . the long slow strata piled to rest
    it on [. . .]. (78)

Whitman's source for these ideas is the so-called nebular hypothesis, advanced by Kant and Laplace: the idea that "the Sun and planets of the solar system might originate by condensation from some thin primordial matter" under the influence of the forces of gravitation.[104] The hypothesis was popularized in America by Robert Chambers's *Vestiges of the Natural History of Creation* (1844), an avowed attempt to "connect the natural sciences into a history of creation" and a book Whitman appears to have been familiar with.[105] By observing nebulae, blurred clusters of stars in the night sky, it is possible, Chambers explains, to gain "a glimpse of the process through which a sun goes between its original condition, as a mass of diffused nebulous matter, and its full-formed state as a compact body."[106] The discovery of a uniform process of organic creation and the popularization of astronomy in the mid-nineteenth century allowed the popular comprehension of a universe "bound up in one chain, interwoven in one web of mutual relation and harmonious agreement, subjected to one pervading influence."[107] Collapsing the boundaries of time and space, Whitman locates his embryo as an instance of zygotic cohering analogous to, and part of, the cohering of suns and planets from the lethargic mists and the creation of the earth's strata from out of the "foetid carbon" (78).

The draft for this section of "Song of Myself" is in the notebook, "Poem Incarnating the Mind":

Amelioration is the blood that runs through the body of the universe.—I do not lag.—I do not hasten—I bide my hour over billions of billions of years. I exist in the void that takes uncounted time and coheres to a nebula, and in further time cohering to an orb, marches, gladly round, a beautiful tangible creature, in her place in the processions of God . . . my right hand is time, and my left is space—both are ample—a few quintillions of cycles, a few sextillions of cubic leagues, are not of importance to me—what I shall attain to I can never tell, for there is something that underlies me, of whom I am a part and instrument. (NUPM 1:104–5)

"Amelioration" links Whitman's stargazing to the moral, reforming impulse of the so-called Harmonists and, in particular, to the work of Andrew Jackson Davis. "The mind cannot be chained!" Davis declares in The Principles of Nature (1852): "not satisfied with the investigation of terrestrial things, it has soared to the heavens and counted the stars. It has familiarized itself with the motions of the planets, given names to laws that control the universe."[108] For Davis, bringing the mind to a rational understanding of organic process promises a "social resurrection," since "the voices and supplications of Nature can not be hushed." Nature, "dwelling within living forms, speaks, and loudly calls for amelioration from ignorance, vice, imbecility, and every species of social iniquity, transgression, and disorganization."[109] (The term "amelioration," which has both medical and religious meanings, occurs a total of thirteen times in The Principles of Nature.) Davis provides an ecstatic, religious version of the nebular hypothesis, with "circles" of suns evolving from a "magnificent nebulous Zone" and revolving around a "GREAT CEN-TRE," a "Vortex, breathing forth a system of concentric circles of suns and systems of suns."[110] Whitman combines the voices of amateur astronomer and Harmonist:

I open my scuttle at night and see the far-sprinkled systems,
[. . . . .]

My sun has his sun, and round him obediently wheels,
He joins with his partners a group of superior circuit,
And greater sets follow, making specks of the greatest inside them.
  (*LG* 79)

Why the persistent stargazing, even at the lowest levels of the demo-cratic mass? Why the resort to "myriads of spheres" after the brutish kaboo, the floating sacs? The nebular hypothesis is satisfying to a writer attempting a boldly syncretic poem like "Song of Myself" because it describes how confused and chaotic material gains form and substance. To a complex, "advanced civilisation," the physical sciences promise the assur-ance of "the invariability of natural laws, amid the perplexities of ceaseless change."[111] For Davis, the principles of nature are to be applied to the busi-ness of social reform, but they also serve a more individual, therapeu-tic purpose. "Let us, if possible, escape from cities," writes another Harmonist, Marx Edgeworth Lazarus, "from the social maelstroms and treadmills of civilized industry."[112] We will know when we are "healed" when "calm and unreproved we can press our cheek to our mother earth's great breast, and feel our heart answer to the pulses of her life."[113] Stargaz-ing with the Harmonists serves multiple functions for Whitman: escape from social degradation, the consolation of a secure place in the cosmos, and the promise of social amelioration.

The problem, I think, is that Whitman by 1855 had no point of political agency. He had been banished from his place in the Democratic Party for his Free-Soil heresy, and the Free-Soil movement itself had been defeated. Democratic politics had turned decisively to the slavery question rather than social reform.[114] Whitman's Locofoco politics was absorbed into the cry for Free-Soil and spent itself in it. For all the taunts aimed at him by his rivals, the respectable Brooklyn editor never established links with the shirt-less Democracy. The simple, baleful fact is that the cosmos, "the far-sprin-kled systems" of suns, is the only organizational principle Whitman can find to appeal to. Herder's "Dialogue on Metempsychosis" advises, "The system which [Newton] constructed out of stars and suns—let that be to you the fabric of your immortality, of an ever-during progress and upward flight. . . . O! how great is the dwelling in which the Creator has placed me, and O, how fair! . . . My course is the path of the All of worlds."[115] This becomes, in "Song of Myself," a series of cosmic affirmations:

> O suns . . . . O grass of graves . . . . O perpetual transfers and
>   promotions [. . .]. (*LG* 84)

> It is not chaos or death . . . . it is form and union and plan . . . . it is
>   eternal life . . . . it is happiness. (85)

It's the tone of voice as much as the high-flown abstraction that compels attention here. A long time ago, Perry Miller pointed out that, if examined closely, Whitman's self-consciously oracular pronouncements stem not from "a mood of serene self-possession and self-assurance" but from "a per-vasive self-distrust. There is a nervous instability at the bottom of the histri-onic ostentation."[116] That combination of anxiety and celebration seems to me to define Whitman's distinctive tone, a tone that is shaped by the conflictual ideological pattern of the 1840s.

The rhetoric of affirmation through lament is what Sacvan Bercovitch describes as "the jeremiad formula," a structure derived from the political sermons of New England Puritanism.[117] Thriving on the very "discrepancy between appearance and promise" in American life, the jeremiad works to convert a sense of declension into "a ritual of cultural aspiration."[118] It is just because so much has been promised to a chosen people in a new world that, whatever the actual failings of American society, they can be repaired and the covenant redeemed. A weary Whitman offers the reader this promise of redemption in the closing sections of "Song of Myself."

In the absence of collective bonds, with the failure of politics, everyone must travel the road of life alone, although Whitman makes an offer of com-panionship—paradoxically as he starts to take his leave of us—in the mixed diction he has perfected as his ambiguous means of registering class contention and class mingling:

> Shoulder your duds, and I will mine, and let us hasten forth;
> Wonderful cities and free nations we shall fetch as we go. (*LG* 80)

The proposed journey is to be undertaken by "each man and each woman of you." The whole of America is to join Whitman on the journey into futurity and its "limitless" prospect of growth and development, a prospect that is shot through with the rarified tone of Manifest Destiny—a tone that welcomes imperial expansion as Providential plan, evolutionary law, and cosmic necessity. Menippus has departed and Jeremiah has taken his place. The many sweat while the few idly own; predatory lawyers and capitalists baton on the workers and suck them dry. But in America, for those who labor honestly, all things are still possible.

The linguistic textures of the verse, however, tell another story: a story of conflicting levels of language and contending social classes. "Duds," meaning clothes and by extension personal goods, is a cant word originating in early modern England; Thomas Harman, in *A Caveat for Common Cursitors* (1566), cites it as an example of the language of "bawdy beggars and vain vagabonds."[119] (Whitman may have picked the word up from Robert Burns's poem "The Jolly Beggars," which consists of a series of airs sung by "a merry core / O' randie, gangrel bodies" who "paw[n] their duds" to buy drink.[120]) To "hasten forth" returns us from the argot of thieves and vagrants to the upper registers of literary language, where it carries a flavor of biblical solemnity and archaism. (Hawthorne uses the phrase in "The New Adam and Eve" (1843), placing "our first parents" in "the heart of a modern city" and telling them to "[h]asten forth with your native innocence, . . . lest another fallen race be propagated."[121]) Whitman's diction in the closing sections of "Song of Myself" continues to oscillate between the coarse and the fine, riverbank and perfumed saloon.

At final parting, Whitman seems to want to reassure us, and himself, that the fancy words he has been using—his promulges, accoucheurs, and debouches—do not mean he is "stuck up," out of place. "The spotted hawk swoops by and accuses me . . . . he complains of my gab and my loitering." The hawk complains twice over, with the vulgar "gab" and with the more literary "loitering," continuing the poem's seriocomic mixture to the end. Whitman backpedals:

I too am not a bit tamed . . . . I too am untranslatable,
I sound my barbaric yawp over the roofs of the world. (*LG* 85)

Whitman, the reader of dictionaries, is playing a complicated game here. According to the 1933 edition of *The Oxford English Dictionary*, "Yawp" (or yaulpe, yolp[e], yalp, yope) is a dialect word of echoic origin; it means "[t]o shout or exclaim hoarsely, to yelp, as a dog; to cry harshly or querulously, as a bird." Whitman so identifies with the untamed bird that he yawps in mimicry of it, with a sound that is "untranslatable" in that it is pure sound: language, as it were, in a state of nature. "Yawp" is all signifier, material mark, naked utterance. As such, it attracts "barbaric": "uncultured, uncivilized, unpolished, rude, rough, wild, savage." "Barbaric" derives from another echoic word, *barbar*, the Greek approximation of the crude sounds made by non-Greeks, which came to stand for everything "foreign, non-Hellenic," "outlandish, rude, brutal." (Whitman could have picked up the word and the context from Carlyle's *On Heroes, Hero-Worship, and the Heroic in History*, which refers to Mohammad as "[a]n uncultured semi-barbarous Son of Nature"—certainly how Whitman sometimes liked to present himself in opposition to polished gentlemen.)[122] But all this is misleading to the extent that Whitman, with "yawp," is also using a signifier embedded in a set of literary and cultural signifieds, a cluster of signs associated with southwestern and Yankee humor. *The Oxford English Dictionary* gives three citations, the first from Joseph Holt Ingraham's *The South-West (A Narrative of Travels)* (New York: Harper, 1835): "Hold your yaup, you youngster you." The following year, the word is put into the mouth of Sam Slick, the Yankee peddler in Thomas Chandler Haliburton's *The Clockmaker, or, the Sayings and Doings of Samuel Slick of Slicksville* (1836): "They stand starin and yawpin, all eyes and mouth." The success of Sam Slick spurred Anna Sophia Stephens to produce *High Life in New York* (1844), the story of Sam's Yankee brother Jonathan: "He looked around as if he wanted to say something . . . but I told him to go ahead and hold his yop."

"You shall no longer take things at second or third hand," Whitman began by promising us, "nor look through the eyes of the dead . . . . nor feed on the spectres in books" (*LG* 26). But far from being "natural" and "original" in the sense intended by its author, "Song of Myself" ends with a cannibalized literature—literature feeding on itself in the closed circuits, the dense networks of cultural reference. Within this textual system, a struggle for power and authority has taken place, a struggle that forces Whitman's language into bizarre and contorted shapes: the shapes of cosmic amelioration and class conflict, bardic utterance and Locofoco abuse. Small wonder, then, that Whitman should end by imagining his own organic decomposition, imagining his body breaking up in "vapour" and "dusk," in "dirt" and "grass," and so eventually entering into our bodies to "filter and fibre [our] blood" (86). Whitman notes in the "Talbot Wilson" notebook how "[d]ifferent objects" decay and "by the chemistry of nature, their bodies are [turned] into spears of grass" (*TW* 24). On the following page, he writes,

> Bring all the art and
> science of the world, and
> baffle and humble it with
> one spear of grass (*TW* 25)

The linguistic admixtures of the text are translated into the mixtures of atomic particles in a last act of defiance of cultural authority and class dominance. Whitman will not "descend among professors and capitalists" (65). Instead,

> I follow   (animals and birds,)
> *Literature is full of*
>   perfumes
> (criticism on *Myself*) (107)

"Song of Myself" presents us with a lower-middle-class autodidact whose identity is fractured by the struggle to reconcile national identity and class division, a contradiction insouciantly admitted ("do I contradict myself?") but scarcely overcome. Short of the real advent of the millennium of liberty, how could it be? The pathos of the poem's ending, surely one of the most sustained and tender of all poetic leave-takings, derives from a political hope for equality nourished on both idealism and bitterness, an individual hope that, in its isolation, reaches out for a companion in hope:

> Failing to fetch me at first keep encouraged,
> Missing me one place search another,
> I stop some where waiting for you (*LG* 86)

Whitman cannot bear to end his song—now contending, now mingling—with so much as a full stop.

POSTSCRIPT: MATERIAL RESISTANCE

Language, in Whitman's poetry, is treated in a new way. A long time ago now, Constance Rourke noted how Whitman "used language as a new and plastic and even comical medium," one in which effects of disjunction and incongruity between linguistic registers are exploited for the purposes of humor.[1] The fundamentally humorous approach Whitman takes toward language involves seeing the linguistic medium as a substance that can be worked over: bent with a mechanic rudeness into contorted shapes or smoothed out by genteel accents. Language in Whitman appears as a substance that—like paint on a modern artist's canvas—has been heavily worked, the marks of its facture left conspicuously visible. Roy Harvey Pearce takes this perception a step further, claiming that Whitman "invents modern poetry" through his realization that the linguistic medium has a kind of "'life' of its own."[2] More recently, Jerome McGann has written of Whitman's "immersion in the material resistance of language."[3] We get a sense of that immersion when Whitman describes his body as being composed of "loveroot, silkthread, crotch and vine," or when he tells us that he is "stucco'd with quadrupeds and birds," or when he sounds his "barbaric yawp" over the roofs of the world (*LG* 25, 55, 85). Whitman's language offers an aesthetic seduction, savoring as it does the phenomenal aspects of words—the crunchy texture of consonants ("gneiss and coal and fruits and grains and esculent roots") as well as the seductive play of long and short vowel sounds ("only the lull I like, the hum of your valved voice"). With its phonemic patterning and its restless foraging among dictionaries and lexicons, the poetry consistently foregrounds what Roland Barthes famously called the "materiality of the signifier."[4]

But how are we to account for that beguiling materiality? Whitman shares with other romantic poets a fascination with *Bildungskraft*, with the productive activity of the poet: mimesis as *poiesis*, or making. Tzvetvan Todorov describes Romantic aesthetics as giving a special emphasis to the "necessary internal coherence" of the poetic artifact, seeing in the organic form of the poem what Wilhelm Von Humboldt called a "higher linguistic power" than the merely expressive or referential.[5] Michel Foucault writes of how the findings of German comparative philology resulted in the early nineteenth century in a shift from the linguistic analysis of representation to a concern with intrinsic verbal elements, so that language becomes, for the first time, an object, an "autonomous organic structure."[6] Words are now, Foucault observes, "weighed down with their own material history." Language ceases to be "transparent to its representations" and undergoes a "thickening," taking on "a peculiar heaviness."[7]

As an apprentice printer who held the shapes of words in his hands, Whitman, of course, knew about the materiality of the signifier in a particularly concrete sense. This brings us to another explanation for the weight and density of his words: "the explosion of text that accompanies the conversion to a market society in the United States."[8] In the torrent of "[a]lmanacs, cheap newspapers, story papers, popular novels, sensational nonfiction and sentimental journalism" that poured from the presses of metropolitan centers like New York, words, heavily inked and variously formed, shouted for the attention of the reading public. The origins of the materiality of the signifier might thus be found in the "repetitiveness, autonomization, and commodification" of language in the popular press.[9]

Another broad cultural development, alongside that of commercial printing, is the growth of the publishing market itself. As R. Jackson Wilson notes, the literary marketplace seems to offer writers "a radical autonomy," a bracing independence from the requirements of patrons or literary institutions: the market creates "a world composed only of the author and the public, with language itself as the only link between them."[10] The paradoxical outcome of the author's new relationship to the marketplace is that language becomes both an autonomous field for experiment, opening the possibility of forging an individual "style," and a commodity subject to the ruthless calculus of exchange.

All these factors—the more or less simultaneous growth of philology, of a commercial print culture, and of the literary market—undoubtedly bear down on language and lend it a new materiality. But what "Song of Myself" reveals, I think, is the influence of what Foucault calls "constant factors of attrition and admixture."[11] Language in Whitman's poem appears as something that both mutates at the lower levels of common speech and appears as a system imposed from above, "a discourse frozen in its own ritual and pomp."[12] And this chafing of linguistic strata against each other was underway, insistently and ineluctably, in Whitman's time and place.

"Washes and razors for foofoos," Whitman declares, abruptly, in "Song of Myself," "for me freckles and a bristling beard" (*LG* 46). In *A Glance at New York*, the genteel Harry Gordon conducts his friend George Parsells to what he calls "the renouned" Loafer's Paradise, "an abode of many worthies"—in the company of Mose, the Bowery b'hoy (Baker 179).

MOSE. (*to Harry, pointing after Loafers*) Them's foo-foos!
GEORGE. What's foo-foos?
MOSE. Why foo-foos is outsiders, and outsiders is foo-foos.
GEORGE. I'm as wise now as ever.
MOSE. Well, as you're a greenhorn, I'll enlighten you. A foo-foo, or outsider, is a chap wot can't come de big figure.
GEORGE. What's the big figure?
MOSE. The big figure here, is three cents for a glass of grog and a night's lodging. (179–80)

The comedy here is had at the expense of George, the polite interlocutor, whose efforts to understand Mose's language are undermined by a potentially infinite regress of meaning, in which one slang term can be fully explained only by another, and that by another. In the clash of class registers, "foo-foos" retains a kind of barbaric innocence, a heavily marked materiality. It is concrete utterance—pure, bewildering, enchanting sound—but its phonemes and their graphic representation are saturated with a particular social existence, a deeply felt, deeply alien life. For Mose, a "foofoo" is someone belonging to the class fraction below the artisan: a lower-class idler or corner lounger, who will "snooze in the market" because he cannot afford a night's lodging (181). For Whitman, "foofoo" refers to those "genteel spirits," denounced in the "Talbot Wilson" notebook, who insist he remove his "bristly beard" with "washes and razors" (*TW* 62). In both cases, the slang word jars against the stiffness and pedantry of the literary, creating an effect of friction between "two voices, two world views, two languages."[13]

Although he doesn't elaborate on the point, Mikhail Bakhtin makes the tantalizing suggestion that when one language rubs up against another in this way, "a feeling for the materiality of language" is produced.[14] This feeling is the result of a certain recession of the referential function, with the word now drawing attention to itself as word rather than simply pointing immediately and transparently to an idea or thing. In the revealed space between the word and its object, "another's word, another's accent intrudes," and "a mantle of materiality" is cast over the signifier.[15] The actual outsiders glimpsed by Mose at the edges of Baker's stage recede into the distance, and we are left with the signs of class in all their alienating exteriority, their hard-to-decipher social existence.

Whitman's dialogism, I have been arguing, stems from his position as a lower-middle-class autodidact: a language user caught in the shifting space between the plebeian "blab" of the "pave" and the upper-class "promenade." If Whitman, as Pearce argues, "invents modern poetry," then this invention is made not merely through his realization that the linguistic medium has a "'life' of its own" but through an awareness of the different class accents in which that life is expressed.

The invention comes at a high price, however—the price of social and political isolation. The loneliness of the speaker in the closing sections of "Song of Myself" is bound up with a feeling of nostalgia, of yearning for a more settled, less ambiguous class location: a longing for rural folkways and hallowed patterns of labor, for "the young mechanic," the "woodman that takes his axe and jug with him," "[t]he farmboy ploughing the field" (*LG* 82). In the dusk, Whitman waits by the road for them, having shouldered his duds and hastened forth—still stranded between conflicting languages and classes, still speaking with a forked tongue.

NOTES

INTRODUCTION

1. R. W. B. Lewis, *American Adam*, 1.
2. Jerome Loving, *Walt Whitman*, 178.
3. David S. Reynolds, *Beneath the American Renaissance*, 313; Betsy Erkkila, *Whitman the Political Poet*, 4. Erkkila goes on to describe Whitman as a "historically specific poet with roots in working-class culture in Brooklyn and New York" (69). Christopher Beach, in *The Politics of Distinction*, asserts that Whitman's bodily self-presentation is "clearly marked as one of working-class or lower-class origin," although this marking is done "without any overt declaration of class-based sympathies" (180).
4. Richard B. Stott, *Workers in the Metropolis*, 264.
5. See, for example, Kenneth Cmiel, *Democratic Eloquence: The Fight over Popular Speech in Nineteenth-Century America*; Hans Bergmann, *God in the Street: New York Writing from the Penny Press to Melville*; Isabelle Lehuu, *Carnival on the Page: Popular Print Media in Antebellum America*; Edward Widmer, *Young America: The Flowering of Democracy in New York City*; Anthony Gronowicz, *Race and Class Politics in New York City before the Civil War*. Among studies that locate Whitman firmly within the antebellum period, see Joseph Jay Rubin, *The Historic Walt Whitman*, and David S. Reynolds, *Walt Whitman's America: A Cultural Biography*.
6. Donald Pease, "Walt Whitman's Revisionary Democracy," 151.
7. Pease, "Walt Whitman's Revisionary Democracy," 152, 153. For a similar description of Whitman as an honest "broker" between the upper-middle-class culture of Broadway and the working-class culture of the Bowery, see M. Wynn Thomas, "Whitman's Tale of Two Cities," 648.
8. See James Perrin Warren, *Walt Whitman's Language Experiment*, 7–33.
9. Edwin Fussell, *Lucifer in Harness: American Meter, Metaphor, and Diction*, 123.
10. Lewis, *American Adam*, 5, 9. In *Walt Whitman's Language Experiment*, Warren provides a detailed analysis of loan words and word formations in Whitman but argues that these designate "a kind of spiritual democracy, a mass movement of progressive social spirits toward perfect linguistic and political liberty"—a movement that has neither a defined historical context nor any actual members (50). In *Imagining Language in America: From the Revolution to the Civil War*, Michael P.

Kramer discusses Whitman's linguistic thought but refers only glancingly to its "antielitist, antigenteel aspect"; see 90–115, esp. 95. Notable exceptions to the dehistoricizing and depoliticizing of Whitman's style are Betsy Erkkila, "Walt Whitman: The Politics of Language," and Jonathan Arac, "Whitman and Problems of the Vernacular."

11. John P. McWilliams, Jr., *The American Epic: Transforming a Genre, 1770–1860*, 223, 225.

12. On the Locofocos, see F. Byrdsall, *The History of the Loco-Foco, or Equal Rights Party*; Arthur M. Schlesinger, Jr., *The Age of Jackson*, 191–209; Charles Sellers, *The Market Revolution: Jacksonian America, 1815–1846*, 352.

13. Strong, *The Diary of George Templeton Strong*, vol. 1, 62.

14. James Russell Lowell, "Emerson the Lecturer," 351.

15. Donald M. Scott, "Popular Lecture and the Creation of a Public," 801. See also Mary Kupiec Cayton, "The Making of an American Prophet."

16. Ralph Waldo Emerson, "The Poet," 349.

17. Lowell, "Emerson the Lecturer," 355. Whitman found the lecture "one of the richest and most beautiful compositions, both for its matter and style" that he had "ever heard anywhere, at any time" (*J1* 44).

18. Emerson, *Journals and Miscellaneous Notebooks*, vol. 7, 265.

19. Reynolds, *Beneath the American Renaissance*, 444.

20. Reynolds, *Walt Whitman's America*, 308. See also Isabelle Lehuu, *Carnival on the Page: Popular Print Media in Antebellum America*, for a description of the "heteroglot exuberance of the carnivalesque print culture from the 1830s to the 1850s" (11). Jackson Lears describes the "carnivalesque charge" of an "emerging consumer economy" in the antebellum period in *Fables of Abundance: A Cultural History of Advertising in America*, 46–63, esp. 51.

21. Gary Saul Morson, introduction, 227. For a rejoinder to Morson, see Ken Hirschkop and David Shepperd, "Bakhtin and the Politics of Criticism," 116–18; see also Ken Hirschkop, *Mikhail Bakhtin: An Aesthetic for Democracy*, 7–10.

22. Hirschkop, *Mikhail Bakhtin*, 3.

23. For a rather different conception of Whitman's divided voice, see Richard Pascal's "'Dimes on the Eyes': Walt Whitman and the Pursuit of Wealth in America." Pascal argues that Whitman "attempts, sometimes within the same poem or essay, to be America's sternly watchful doomsayer as well as its exuberant booster," noting the alarming manner in which Whitman can disrupt a "glowing

panegyric" with a "diatribe" (146, 152). But, having described a "tension" between the two voices, Pascal moves too quickly to reconcile them, positing Whitman's "return to natural spontaneity" as the solution to the materialism of American capitalism (170). I argue in this book that the divided voice remains a constant throughout *Leaves of Grass* and that specifying the different voices more closely in terms of their particular historical resonance in the political and cultural struggles of the antebellum period allows us to hear their continued contention.

24. Whitman, like many other young men in the expanding metropolis, looked to culture both as a symbol of upward mobility and as a practical means of achieving the "character" necessary for success in life. When, in 1856, Whitman published a *Life Illustrated* article on language, with the title "America's Mightiest Inheritance," he included an "Appendant for Working People, Young Men and Women, and for Boys and Girls," which included "*A few Foreign Words, mostly French, put down Suggestively*"—words such as *Allons* ("Let us go"), *nonchalance* ("Easy, without bashfulness or formality"), *Ami/Amie* ("Dear Friend"), *canaille* ("Dirty low people") (*NYD* 61–62). The very choice of words here is calculated to both enhance social motion and draw distinctions.

25. Peter G. Buckley, "Culture, Class, and Place in Antebellum New York," 34.

26. I borrow these terms from R. Jackson Wilson, *Figures of Speech: American Writers and the Literary Marketplace*, 3. Antonio Gramsci's words are worth recalling, as they apply with particular force to Whitman's situation:

> When one's conception of the world is not critical and coherent but
> disjointed and episodic, one belongs simultaneously to a multiplicity of mass
> human groups. The personality is strangely composite. . . . The starting point
> of critical elaboration is the consciousness of what one really is, and is
> "knowing thyself" as a product of the historical process to date which has
> deposited in you an infinity of traces, without leaving an inventory. (324)

If *Leaves of Grass* is "disjointed" and "episodic" and Whitman's personality "strangely composite," then these features reflect the instabilities and blurred boundaries of Whitman's class location, as well as what can seem like an "infinity" of historical and textual traces.

27. Mikhail Bakhtin, "Discourse in the Novel," 293.

28. Thomas Augst, "Antebellum Authorship," 360.

29. Augst, *Clerk's Tale*, 15.

30. William E. Channing, "Self-Culture," 407. An idea of the somewhat contorted and

perplexed contours of self-improvement can be gained from reading the garbled quotation from Channing in *The American Gentleman's Guide to Politeness and Fashion*, first published in 1850, by Margaret Cockburn Conkling, who used the pseudonym Henry Lunettes. The wife of a prominent New York jurist, Conkling presented a series of "letters" to some "dear nephews," in which the broadly conceived, even transcendental, goals of self-culture jar against more mundane aspirations for self-improvement, such as these: "Decorum in the presence of Ladies—Carrying the Hat, ease of Attitude, etc.—Benefits of habitual Self-Restraint—Habits at Table—Eating with a Knife—Soiling the Lips, Picking the Teeth, etc., etc." (xx). On the distinction between self-culture and self-improvement, see John G. Cawelti, *Apostles of the Self-Made Man*, 80–85; on the self-culture movement as an effort by the rising middle classes to "come to grips with the exigencies of nascent industrial capitalism," see Ronald J. Zboray, *Fictive People*, 129–31, esp. 129.

31. Zboray, *Fictive People*, 129. Zboray points out that literary culture was not within the means of all Americans. Despite advances in printing technology and distribution, books remained essentially luxury items: at one dollar, the cost of a hardcover book represented a day's work for a skilled male worker, four days for a female worker. Even fifty-cent paperback editions of American authors were "out of reach to most working-class readers" (12). The chief beneficiaries of the publishing boom were members of the "native-born, lower middle class" in the northeastern cities—those men and women who, like Whitman, sought upward mobility and personal improvement (133). The "culture of reprinting" was a "cultural diaspora" rather than a "unified print culture" (134, 15).

32. Michel de Certeau, *Practice*, 171.

33. De Certeau, *Practice*, 171.

34. De Certeau, *Practice*, 169.

35. De Certeau, *Practice*, 174.

36. Meredith L. McGill, *American Literature*, 285n38.

37. Paul Zweig, *Walt Whitman*, 153.

38. Augst, *Clerk's Tale*, 37.

39. Augst, *Clerk's Tale*, 60.

40. In this context, Emerson's well-known description of *Leaves of Grass* as a "combination of the *Bhagavad-Gita* and the New York *Herald*" registers a twinge of educated, middle-class unease at such promiscuous intermingling. See Bliss Perry, *Walt Whitman*, 276n1.

1. SEX, CLASS, AND COMMERCE

1. Ed Folsom, *Walt Whitman's Native Representations*, 145.

2. F. O. Matthiessen, *American Renaissance*, 542, 542–43. Whitman's appropriation by the American left begins with the socialist Horace L. Traubel, who was Whitman's amanuensis after 1888 and his literary executor. Whitman gave equivocal support to Traubel's ideas but disconcertingly included Andrew Carnegie in the range of his democratic sympathy. On Whitman and Traubel, see David S. Reynolds, *Walt Whitman's America*, 556–59. On Whitman's adoption by the Greenwich Village intellectuals of the 1910s and 1920s, see Edward Abrahams, *The Lyrical Left: Randolph Bourne, Alfred Stieglitz, and the Origins of Cultural Radicalism in America*, 32; John Patrick Diggins, *The Rise and Fall of the American Left*, 94; see also Casey Nelson Blake, *Beloved Community: The Cultural Criticism of Randolph Bourne, Van Wyck Brooks, Waldo Frank, and Lewis Mumford*, 3, 31, 123–25, 173. On Whitman's revival as a culture hero of the left in the 1930s via the Communist Party's promotion of "proletarian" literature, see Jonathan Arac, "F. O. Matthiessen: Authorizing an American Renaissance," 90–111; Daniel Aaron, *Writers on the Left: Episodes in American Literary Communism*, 6–7; Leslie Fiedler, "Images of Walt Whitman," 55–73. See also Bryan K. Gorman, "'Heroic Spiritual Grandfather': Whitman, Sexuality, and the American Left, 1890–1940." More recent efforts to link Whitman with the working-class politics of the antebellum period are Joseph Fichtelberg, *Critical Fictions: Sentiment and the American Market*, 160–200, and Andrew C. Higgins, "Wage Slavery and the Composition of *Leaves of Grass*."

3. On the "bachelor subculture" of antebellum New York City, see Sean Wilentz, *Chants Democratic: New York City and the Rise of the American Working Class, 1788–1850*, 53–60; Elliott J. Gorn, "'Good-Bye Boys, I Die a True American': Homicide, Nativism, and Working Class Culture in Antebellum New York City."

4. On liminality, see Victor S. Turner, *Drama, Fields, and Metaphors: Symbolic Action in Human Society*, 231–71. On the connection between liminality and the market, see Turner, *From Ritual to Theatre: The Human Seriousness of Play*, 40; Jean-Christophe Agnew, *Worlds Apart: The Market and the Theater in Anglo-American Thought*, 17–27.

5. On the artisan system, see Wilentz, *Chants Democratic*, 23–60.

6. On the transformation of the artisan system by "metropolitan industrialization," see Wilentz, *Chants Democratic*, 107–42. See also Bruce Laurie, *Artisans into Workers: Labor in Nineteenth-Century America*, 14–41; Charles Sellers, *The Market Revolution*, 23–27.

7. Unsigned review of *Leaves of Grass, New York Daily News*.

8. "Notes on New Books," unsigned review of *Leaves of Grass, Washington Daily National Intelligencer*.

9. Charles H. Haswell, *Reminiscences of an Octogenarian of the City of New York*, 270–71; George G. Foster, *New York by Gas-Light*, 174, 169–77. See also Foster, *New York in Slices*, 43–47. On the Bowery b'hoy, see Alvin F. Harlow, *Old Bowery Days*, 190–256. For a survey of the historical sources, see Richard M. Dorson, "Mose the Far-Famed and World-Renowned." See also Wilentz, *Chants Democratic*, 300–301; Christine Stansell, *City of Women: Sex and Class in New York*, 89–91; Eric Lott, *Love and Theft: Blackface Minstrelsy and the American Working Class*, 81–87; Rosemarie K. Bank, *Theatre Culture in America*, 85–92.

10. Of Whitman's self-identification with the b'hoy, David S. Reynolds claims in *Beneath the American Renaissance* that *Leaves of Grass* grows "directly" from the b'hoy's "boisterous working-class consciousness" (513). For Richard B. Stott, in *Workers in the Metropolis*, Whitman's "celebrations of the city's concrete life . . . touch on key aspects of working-class culture" (275). It is these allied notions of a direct relation between class identity and literary expression and of a homogeneous working-class consciousness that I want to question here. For a more nuanced reading of Whitman's class location, see Peter G. Buckley, "Culture, Class, and Place in Antebellum New York."

11. Haswell, *Reminiscences*, 270–71.

12. Wilentz, *Chants Democratic*, 137, 138.

13. Wilentz, *Chants Democratic*, 190.

14. Wilentz, *Chants Democratic*, 139.

15. Stansell, *City of Women*, 91. See also Reynolds, *Beneath the American Renaissance*, 463.

16. On the resistance of "premodern" work habits to industrialization, see Herbert G. Gutman, *Work, Culture, and Society in Industrializing America*, 19–32. For the notion of "working class traditionalism" as an "indefatigably autonomous culture" opposed to middle-class temperance and "industrial morality," see Bruce Laurie, *Working People of Philadelphia*, 53–66, esp. 54. For an important qualification to the notion that class cultures are autonomous and bounded entities, see Gorn, "'Good-Bye Boys,'" 406–8.

17. Foster, *New York by Gas-Light*, 177.

18. Foster, *New York in Slices*, 44.

19. Foster, *New York in Slices*, 47, 45.

20. Thomas, *The Lunar Light of Whitman's Poetry*, 651.

21. For the notion of the "moral economy," see E. P. Thompson, "The Moral Economy of the English Crowd in the Eighteenth Century." On the "rifts of class" forming within the artisan system by the 1830s, see Wilentz, *Chants Democratic*, 96, 101–3.

22. Reynolds, *Beneath the American Renaissance*, 512.

23. Cornelius Mathews, *A Pen-and-Ink Panorama of New York City*, 137. Charles MacKay observes that the volunteer firemen of the city popularly identified with the b'hoys are "mostly youths engaged during the day in various handicrafts and mechanical trades, with a sprinkling of clerks and shopmen" (35).

24. Bank, *Theatre Culture*, 78. On the new status of clerks, see Allan S. Horlick, *Country Boys and Merchant Princes*; Caroll Smith-Rosenberg, *Disorderly Conduct*, 80–81; Stuart M. Blumin, *The Emergence of the Middle Class*, 66–107. In *The Clerk's Tale*, Thomas Augst provides a detailed analysis—and a rich evocation—of the "moral drama" inherent in the lives of these "rootless and restless young men becoming civilized while pursuing democratic freedoms in the midst of the market revolution" (3).

25. Arno J. Mayer, "The Lower Middle Class as Historical Problem," 423.

26. Alexis de Tocqueville, *Democracy in America*, 255.

27. Dion Boucicault, *The Poor of New York*, 40–41.

28. Turner, *The Ritual Process*, 95.

29. Mayer, "Lower Middle Class," 409, 418.

30. My information on Whitman's family is drawn largely from David S. Reynolds, *Walt Whitman's America*, 7–29.

31. Newton Arvin, *Whitman*, 101.

32. Mathews, *Pen-and-Ink Panorama*, 136.

33. Gorn, "'Good-Bye Boys,'" 408. In "Whitman's Tale of Two Cities," M. Wynn Thomas makes the unusually accurate observation that Whitman operates, in his journalism, "at a point where the respectable working class merged imperceptibly with the lower middle class" (648–49). Thomas follows this with the equally valuable insight that this ambiguous class location inspired Whitman's "wild, transgressive, and creative impulse to mix, to 'intermingle,' to blend" (649). In *The Lunar Light of Whitman's Poetry*, Thomas argues that Whitman attempts, in *Leaves of Grass*, to heal the rifts opened up within artisanal culture by the market

by "graft[ing]" the "mutuality" of artisan republicanism onto the "expansive opportunities" of the "competitive and libertarian free enterprise system," thus producing "the rootedness of authentic selfhood" (30, 63). In *Critical Fictions*, Joseph Fichtelberg refers to Whitman's "ambiguous class position," somewhere between "dependent laborer" and "autonomous agent" (163, 176). Where Thomas sees a grafting of class identities, Fichtelberg argues that Whitman transmutes a fragmented antebellum populace into the image of a regulated capitalist order. Both approaches want to dispense too readily with contradiction and move too quickly away from the fractures and divisions of concrete historical circumstances into the more "harmonious" sphere of literary art. For me, Whitman's redemptive efforts fail, due to the contradictions and ambivalences involved in the market's "expansive opportunities." Much can be learned from that failure, however. Once the point at which classes merge is made more perceptible, it becomes possible to explore the emotional and psychological implications of life in the market economy for the lower middle class and to grasp the full range of creative and political possibilities in Whitman's impulse to intermingle.

34. For an insightful discussion of the novel's interest in "the dilemmas of self-coherence," see Michael Warner, "Whitman Drunk," esp. 36. I have benefited from Jeffrey B. Mason's discussion of how antebellum temperance plays dramatized the "middle-class burden of mobility," in *Melodrama and the Myth of America*, esp. 72.

35. Thomas, "Whitman and the Dreams of Labor," 135.

36. Reprinted in William White, "A Tribute to William Hartshorne: Unrecorded Whitman" (Brooklyn Printer, 555).

37. Walt Whitman, "Wicked Architecture," *Life Illustrated*, July 19, 1856 (*NYD* 92, 94).

38. Paul Zweig, *Walt Whitman: The Making of the Poet*, 136, 137. For the details of Whitman's house building ventures, see Jerome Loving, *Walt Whitman: The Song of Himself*, 180.

39. On the market revolution, see Michael Paul Rogin, *Fathers and Children*, 251–79; Sellers, *Market Revolution*; James Livingston, *Pragmatism and the Political Economy of Cultural Revolution*, 24–31; and Melvyn Stokes and Stephen Conway, *The Market Revolution in America*.

40. Marvin Meyers, *Jacksonian Persuasion*, 133, 136.

41. C. B. Macpherson, *Political Theory of Possessive Individualism*, 55, 57.

42. Sacvan Bercovitch, *Rites of Assent*, 47, 48. In the inflated rhetoric of the popular

press, self-invention presents an inspiring but daunting prospect. An anonymous *Harper's* article, "Success in Life," adumbrates the antebellum success ethic in terms of the distance a man travels from his origins, the wealth he accumulates, the achievement of "a well-disciplined, well-regulated character," and the practice of "familiar virtues; as, for instance, punctuality, prudence, foresight, caution—and yet, also, decision and enterprise" (239). The successful man must also "help on humanity" through an "enlarged benevolence," all the time remembering that "[f]or a bright manhood there is no such word as fail" (238).

43. Zweig, *Walt Whitman*, 96.

44. Karl Marx, *Capital*, vol. 1, 163, 166, 163.

45. Marx, *Capital*, 204.

46. Marx, *Capital*, 164. Whitman's diction converts the abstract and alienating back into the tactile and familiar. According to the *Oxford English Dictionary* (1971), "blab" is an archaic word for "chatter," found in Chaucer and *Piers Plowman*; "sluff" is, appropriately enough, a word of metamorphosis, denoting "the outer or scarf skin periodically cast or shed by a snake," occurring in both Shakespeare's *Henry VI, Part 2* (1593) and Walter Scott's *Kenilworth* (1821). Shakespeare, according to artisanal legend, was regularly read in the workshop to accompany labor. Together, "blab," "sluff," and "clank" evoke the life world—the stability, security, and collective culture—of the artisanal mode of production. I owe this insight to Richard Godden.

47. Doris Sommer, "Supplying Demand: Walt Whitman as the Liberal Self," 74.

48. Marx, *Capital*, 179.

49. Ezra Greenspan, "Some Remarks on the Poetics of 'Participle-Loving Whitman,'" 96. For the idea that Whitman's poetry follows the logic of the commodity, see also Jonathan Arac, "Whitman and Problems of the Vernacular," 55. For more affirmative assessments of Whitman's relation to the market, see Lewis Hyde, *The Gift: Imagination and the Erotic Life of Property*, 160–215, and Livingston, *Pragmatism*, 169–70, 204–6.

50. Quoted from the masthead of the *Long Islander*; see Rubin, *The Historic Walt Whitman*, 37.

51. The following notice for a Locofoco meeting in April 1837 gives a sense of what Sellers terms their "laissez-faire radicalism" and "self-making demand for equal entrepreneurial opportunity"—but also of their appeal to common laborers and artisans (352):

AGAIN TO THE PARK—TO THE PARK.

The People are sovereign.—

They will meet in the Park, rain or shine, on Monday, April 3d, at half past two o'clock, to unite against those moral and political abuses, the curse of paper money, the market and ferry monopolies, and to reform the city government, in order to bring down the high prices of bread, meat, rents, and fuel. (Byrdsall, 135)

52. Betsy Erkkila notes that "by focusing on the problem of monopoly and corporate wealth," Whitman "avoided the potential contradiction between the free-enterprise society he lived in and the harmonious and egalitarian democratic society of his dreams. . . . Envisioning the commercial spirit as an essentially benign, civilizing, and unifying force, Whitman never carried his critique of capitalism to an attack on the concept of free enterprise itself" (*Whitman the Political Poet*, 37, 38). But Whitman's class location made this kind of overt critique impossible: Whitman's is not a "working-class discontent," but what Erkkila later terms an "artisan radicalism" (48, 95). I will argue in what follows that Whitman's poetry offers a subliminal resistance to, and implied critique of, the "freedoms" of the market.

53. Meyers, *Jacksonian Persuasion*, 180.

54. Richard Hofstadter, *The American Political Tradition*, 61.

55. Tocqueville, *Democracy in America*, 253.

56. O. S. Fowler, *Amativeness; Or, Evils and Remedies of Excessive and Perverted Sexuality*, 21.

57. Fowler, *Amativeness*, 22, 23.

58. Fowler, *Amativeness*, 32, 52.

59. Meyers, *Jacksonian Persuasion*, 11. On the fears for personal stability provoked by the Jacksonian market, see Lears, *Fables of Abundance*, 48. On the discourse of antionanism as a symptom of "self-making stress," see Sellers, *Market Revolution*, 245–51. For an account of Whitman's relation to male-purity reformers, see Reynolds, *Whitman's America*, 199–201.

60. See Barker-Benfield, "The Spermatic Economy."

61. In "'Dimes on the Eyes'," Richard Pascal notes how the universe functions for Whitman as "the soundest conceivable capitalist economy. No wise investment, no exuberant human activity, can fail to produce dividends, and loss is impossible" (152). For Pascal, this "transcendent capitalist logic" allows Whitman to posit a "return to natural spontaneity" as the solution to the materialism and

moneygrubbing of American society (160, 170). Although Pascal finds much to approve in Whitman's concern with "being" rather than "having," he finally judges the poetry to be based more on "idealist pomp" than "concrete historical circumstance" (171). By contrast, I argue in what follows that there is a good deal of concrete and particular historical circumstance in *Leaves of Grass*: indeed, the book records the legacy of a series of cultural and political struggles in which Whitman was vitally involved, from Locofoco agitation against monopoly and "aristocracy" to the Free-Soil movement of the late 1840s. In the present chapter, I show how the dark undertow of Whitman's capitalistic rhetoric discloses more of the vicissitudes of fortune in a market society than Pascal allows.

62. Edwin T. Freedley, quoted in Laurie, *Artisans into Workers*, 40.

63. Elaine Scarry, *The Body in Pain*, 248.

64. Marx, *Grundrisse*, 505.

65. Marx, *Capital*, 165.

66. Michael Moon, *Disseminating Whitman*, 75, 59.

67. For a discussion of how eighteenth-century merchants represented loss of fortune in trading enterprises as critical episodes in a history of masculine self-fashioning, see Toby Ditz, "Shipwrecked."

68. Marx, *Capital*, 167, 168.

69. Meyers, *Jacksonian Persuasion*, 137. In "Walt Whitman: The Spermatic Imagination," Harold Aspiz draws attention to the paradox of retention and emission, or saving and spending, in Whitman but without providing an explanation for it. Mark Maslan, in *Whitman Possessed*, provides a detailed analysis of antebellum sexual hygiene authors, including Sylvester Graham and Orson Fowler, and concludes that what unites them is an anxiety about desire, imagined as an external force "assaulting and subjugating the male body" (28). But Maslan does not explain exactly why there should be such an anxiety about the loss of autonomy involved in the assault. Maslan reads sex in "Song of Myself" as straightforwardly celebratory, turning the logic of sexual hygiene against itself to imply that "*surrendering to desire is like surrendering to a man*" (50) and that "*the logic of poetic possession renders self-control counterproductive*" (58). But while Maslan establishes the connection between homoeroticism and poetic inspiration, it's not clear what allows Whitman to evade the prescriptions of the period so easily and so construct a story of "joyful surrender to an overwhelming urge" (59). When Whitman describes his senses as "prurient provokers" (*LG* 53), he uses an adjective that

retains the morally prescriptive sense of desire as troubling and excessive, even as he embraces the possibility of "a new identity." A mood of ambivalence rather than celebration seems to me to structure Whitman's narratives of arousal. For a discussion of Whitman, masturbation, and homosexuality asserting that Whitman's "project" was to subvert male-purity discourse, see Moon, *Disseminating Whitman*, 19–25; for a discussion highlighting Whitman's "ambivalence," see M. Jimmie Killingsworth, *Whitman's Poetry of the Body*, 47–54.

70. W. J. Rorabaugh describes the ritual and social meaning of apprenticeship in early America in *The Craft Apprentice*, 3–15. On the importance of "personal relations" and for a suggestion of the homosocial bonds that sustained apprentices through the transition to industrialization, see 97–112, esp. 104 and 106.

71. On Whitman's explicit phallicism, see E. H. Miller, *Walt Whitman's Poetry*, 124–25.

72. Terry Mulcaire, "Publishing Intimacy in *Leaves of Grass*," 475. The vision of an expanded sensorium consequent on the "supercession of private property" is, of course, a constant theme in Marx, beginning with the hymn to the senses in the *Economic and Philosophical Manuscripts* (1844); see *Early Writings*, 352. In the *Grundrisse*, the idea is traced back to both the Asiatic mode of production and the stage of artisanal production preceding the development of industrial capitalism, where "[t]he individual relates simply to the objective conditions of labor as being his own; [relates] to them as the inorganic nature of his subjectivity . . . a presupposition of his activity just like his skin" (485). Elaine Scarry emphasizes that Marx's political critique of capitalism derives from his conception of "man-as-maker" rather than "man-as-intellect": Marx's moral outrage at capitalism is a protest against "the severing of the worker from his own extended body" (253, 250). Whitman jumps straight from the market's metamorphosis of labor into disembodied processes and structures, back to the artisan-worker projecting sentience into his artifacts without connecting the two sequences—as if the market sprang fully formed from the artisan system, without the mechanism of wage labor and the extraction of surplus value. Otherwise, Whitman's disoriented progress through the market has something of the "metaphysical incredulity of a good craftsman looking at a bad piece of work" that Scarry attributes to Marx (258).

73. Moon, *Disseminating Whitman*, 228n20.

74. Judith N. Shklar, *American Citizenship*, 64.

75. Livingston, "Modern Subjectivity and Consumer Culture," 426; Lears, "Reconsidering Abundance," 460. How you feel about Whitman depends, in crucial respects, on

how you feel about the market. For Sacvan Bercovitch, Whitman is the poet of "the American system," his work characterized by "an unmediated relation between the facts of American life and the ideals of liberal free enterprise." Faced with the market's inadequacies, Whitman turns "for solace and inspiration" to an idealized vision of a market free of conflict, full only of boundless opportunity for self-creation: a market "without confusion or jostling or jam" (*Rites of Assent*, 190, 59). For James Livingston, Whitman's poetry is the harbinger of a consumer culture that offers new imaginative possibilities precisely because its goods are "commodities that necessarily [have] more than local meanings or particular use-values: their profusion complicate[s] and enlarge[s] the perceptible relation between the interior and the exterior of the self." Whitman's "critical edge" is to be found not in "a celebration of artisanal modes of production" but in "the diversity of identifications—and in the weird abstractions—afforded by the new industrial stage of development" (*Pragmatism*, 30–31, 363n32). What's common to both these interpretations is a naive voluntarism, as if Whitman simply took up a position toward the market and stuck to it. What's missing from both views is a sense of Whitman's class location and how that location might contribute to hesitancies and uncertainties in Whitman's response to the political economy of Jacksonian America.

76. On Orestes Brownson, see Christopher Lasch, *The True and Only Heaven*, 203–5. On Thomas Skidmore and the New York Workingmen's movement, see Wilentz, *Chants Democratic*, 172–216.

77. Quoted in Christopher Newfield, "Democracy and Male Homoeroticism," 36. This remarkable—and unremarked—omission means that Newfield's version of Whitman as the poet of radical democracy needs qualifying. For a similar argument that Whitman's poetry is based on "a massive trope of inclusion," see Allen Grossman, "The Poetics of Union in Whitman and Lincoln," esp. 187.

78. Lears, "Reconsidering Abundance," 463.

79. A full transcription of the letter appears in Fredson Bowers, *Whitman's Manuscripts: Leaves of Grass (1860)*, xxxii.

80. Loving, *Walt Whitman*, 239.

2. THE AMERICAN 1848

1. Cornelius Mathews, "The Late Ben. Smith, Loafer," 63.

2. See R. H. Thornton, *An American Glossary*, where seven examples of "loafer" date from 1837, the highest total for any one year.

3. Emerson, "Spiritual Laws," 79.

4. Emerson, "Spiritual Laws," 79, 81.

5. Emerson, "Spiritual Laws," 94. According to Joseph Jay Rubin, Whitman had read the article, "The Philosophy of the Ancient Hindus," published anonymously in Emerson's *Massachusetts Quarterly Review*. The article quotes the *Vishnu Purana*, in H. T. Colebrooke's translation: "[t]he great end of all is Soul: One, pervading, uniform, perfect, preeminent over nature, exempt from birth, growth and decay, omnipresent, undecaying, and unconnected with unrealities, with name, species, and the rest, in time present, past, or to come. The knowledge that this spirit, which is essentially one, is in one's own and in all other bodies, is the great end, or true wisdom, of one who knows the unity and the true principles of things" (416). "Possessed of this (self-knowledge)," the article continues, with a quotation from the *Sankhya Karika*, "soul contemplates at leisure and at ease Nature, (thereby) debarred from prolific change" (419). Whitman's self-improving reading makes even loafing in the grass a spiritual exercise. See Rubin, *Historic Walt Whitman*, 213.

6. Emerson, *Journals*, vol. 7, 174.

7. "New Publications," *Brooklyn Daily Times*, December 17, 1856, 1.

8. Matthiessen, *American Renaissance*, 529.

9. Matthiessen, *American Renaissance*, 529, 530.

10. Matthiessen, *American Renaissance*, 531.

11. Matthiessen, *American Renaissance*, 532.

12. Gay Wilson Allen, *New Walt Whitman Handbook*, 243.

13. Emerson, "The Poet," quoted in Allen, *New Walt Whitman Handbook*, 243.

14. Allen, *New Walt Whitman Handbook*, 245.

15. Allen, *New Walt Whitman Handbook*, 248. Christopher Beach, in *The Politics of Distinction*, adopts a similar approach and terminology to Allen's, inflected with Bakhtinian accents. According to Beach, Whitman could "fully appreciate" the "variety" of New York City's "physical and discursive texture" and with complete "impartiality or neutrality" extend a "cosmic embrace" to "all forms of humanity," as well as "all forms of human discourse" (116, 127, 128). Whitman's "curious melange [sic] of discourses" and the "richness of his linguistic palette" serve the purpose of "capturing the urban heteroglossia of mid-century America" (178, 129). Beach presents a supremely "indifferent" Whitman, one who attempts to avoid being identified with any class interest or any form of cultural "distinc-

tion." David S. Reynolds, in *Walt Whitman's America*, finds the linguistic mixtures emollient, Whitman's talk of the soul "add[ing] philosophical depth to the notion of loafing." Throughout "Song of Myself," for Reynolds, this "cross-penetration of cultural levels" has "an ameliorating effect" (327).

16. Emerson, "Spiritual Laws," 81.

17. Emerson, "Spiritual Laws," 87.

18. Emerson, "Spiritual Laws," 86.

19. Emerson, "Spiritual Laws," 87.

20. Quoted in Floyd Stovall, *Foreground of "Leaves of Grass,"* 290.

21. See D. Mirsky's observation that "[t]he prose idiom Whitman employed in bringing new life to poetry was not the colloquial tongue of the street, the factory or the barracks; it was, rather, the language of printed prose, of newspapers and of popular science" (251).

22. On "latent" and "manifest" class conflict, see Jurgen Habermas, *Legitimation Crisis*, 25–27.

23. "Portico, Number Five," 49.

24. Lawrence Buell, *New England Literary Culture*, 88. On the *Knickerbocker* circle, see Perry Miller, *The Raven and the Whale*, 11–68.

25. William Charvat, *Origins of American Critical Thought*, 1.

26. Hugh Blair, *Lectures on Rhetoric and Belles Lettres*, 216–17.

27. Emerson, "On the Present State of Ethical Criticism," 62.

28. Charvat, *Origins of American Critical Thought*, 47, 112.

29. Sheldon W. Liebman, "The Development of Emerson's Theory of Rhetoric," 181–82, 183. On the efforts by the intelligentsia of the Federalist period to salvage the Augustan classical tradition as the basis for literary standards in America, see Lewis P. Simpson, "Federalism and the Crisis of Literary Order"; Linda K. Kerber, *Federalists in Dissent*, 1–22, 95–134; Dennis E. Baron, *Grammar and Good Taste*, 21–39.

30. William Cullen Bryant, "Poets and Poetry of the English Language" (1826), quoted in Fussell, *Lucifer in Harness*, 13.

31. Fussell, *Lucifer in Harness*, 113.

32. Norman Callan, "Augustan Reflective Poetry," 368, 367.

33. William Cullen Bryant, *Poetical Works*, 18.

34. Bryant, *Poetical Works*, 26.

35. Bryant, *Poetical Works*, 318.

36. Bryant, *Poetical Works*, 319. The nineteen-year-old Whitman wrote like an Augustan Englishman in an article on "Greenwood Cemetery" published in a Long Island newspaper, the *Universalist Union*, in 1839. The article draws a Johnsonian lesson on the "transitory nature of terrestrial objects" from the cemetery: "Here the man of business, whose mind has been distracted by a multitude of perplexing cares, and whose health has been impaired by a series of adverse circumstances, may find in this secluded spot a solace for all his misfortunes" (*J1* 10). Whitman's earliest published verse was also firmly within the neoclassical tradition. "Our Future Lot," which appeared in the *Long-Island Democrat* for October 31, 1838, reproduces the theme of "Thanatopsis," meditating in somber fashion on the fact that "[t]his troubled heart and wondrous form / Must both alike decay" (*EPF* 28). "Fame's Vanity" of the following year is a pale imitation of Gray's "Elegy":

> O, many a panting, noble heart
> > Cherishes in its deep recess
> Th' hope to win renown o'er earth
> > From Glory's priz'd caress. (24)

The poem ends with the speaker reconciled to "live on obscure, unknown" since both "mighty one and lowly wretch" must "sleep on the same earthy couch / A hundred seasons hence" (24). While there are few indications here that the Long Island journalist-poet would go on to become the author of *Leaves of Grass*, I argue below that Whitman retains his Latinate diction, mixed with the vernacular, in what is both a registering of class struggle and a strategy of self-improvement.

37. John Pickering, *A Vocabulary*, 13. Pickering is quoting from, and deferring to, the British *Annual Review*.

38. Pickering, *A Vocabulary*, 17, 19.

39. Pickering, *A Vocabulary*, 153, 55, 57, 173.

40. "The English Language," 214, 215. By 1849, the *North American Review* was still inveighing against the admission into American English of "the whims and oddities, the local customs and prejudices, the political and religious strife, the partial knowledge, and perverse ignorance of the uneducated multitude" ("Bartlett's *Dictionary*," 94). For the Whig elite, linguistic corruption is akin to the supposed political and racial degradations brought about by democracy, with its enfranchisement of "creatures of low and foreign birth" (98).

41. W. A. Jones, "Criticism in America," 243.

42. Cornelius Mathews, *The Politicians* (1840), quoted in Miller, *Raven and Whale*, 93.

43. See Hershel Parker, *Herman Melville: A Biography*, 320. The joke is even more pointed once its artisanal origins in the language of caulking are taken into account. According to E. Cobham Brewer,

> [t]he "devil" is a seam between the garboard-strake and the keel, and to "pay" is to cover [it] with pitch. In former times, when vessels were often careened for repairs, it was difficult to calk and pay this seam before the tide turned. Hence the locution the ship is careened, the devil is exposed, but there is no pitch hot ready, and the tide will turn before the work can be done. (346)

   Melville's Whig exquisite lacks the requisite artisanal language ("pay" deriving from *poix*, the French word for "pitch").

44. Eric Partridge, *Slang: Today and Yesterday*, 16, 18.

45. A. Carnoy, *La Science du Mot* (1927), quoted in Partridge, *Slang*, 14.

46. Jones, "Poetry for the People," 268.

47. Jones, "Poetry for the People," 268.

48. On Whitman and Young America, see Rubin, *Historic Walt Whitman*, 170–73, and Reynolds, *Walt Whitman's America*, 81–82.

49. Mathews, *Man in the Republic*, 69.

50. Mathews, *Man in the Republic*, 69, 70.

51. "Mathews's Poems," 510.

52. On Whitman's early theatergoing, see Rubin, *Historic Walt Whitman*, 29–30.

53. James Kirke Paulding, *The Lion of the West*, 19, 54, 55.

54. Constance Rourke, *American Humor*, 173. On Crockett, see Joseph J. Arpad, introduction, 7–38, and Rourke, *American Humor*, 55–59.

55. H. L. Mencken, *The American Language*, 138, 144.

56. Mencken, *American Language*, 557.

57. Walter Blair, *Native American Humor*, 69.

58. For information on Paulding's career, see Nelson F. Adkins, "James K. Paulding's *Lion of the West*."

59. Paulding, *Lion of the West*, 25, 55, 54.

60. James M. Cox, "Humor of the Old Southwest," 104.

61. Cox, "Humor of the Old Southwest," 106.

62. Cox, "Humor of the Old Southwest," 107.

63. Cox, "Humor of the Old Southwest," 107. The vernacular also increasingly spoke to a gnawing dissatisfaction with the insipidity of genteel culture. An early lecture

by Emerson, "English Literature: Introductory," contains the germ of ideas elaborated on in the "Language" chapter of *Nature*:

> Good writing and brilliant discourse are perpetual allegories. The imagery in discourse which delights all men is that which is drawn from observation of natural processes. It is this which gives that piquancy to the conversation of a strong natured farmer or backwoodsman which all men relish. It is the salt of those semisavages, men of strong understanding, who bring out of the woods into the tameness of refined circles a native way of seeing things, and there speak in metaphors. 'I showed him the back of my hand,' said a backwoodsman, for *I broke friendship with him.* (222)

Emerson evidently felt that Crockett was inappropriately strong meat when it came to publishing his first major work.

64. In his study of Herman Melville, *Subversive Genealogy*, Michael Paul Rogin labeled the period in the wake of the Mexican War "the American 1848," with the intention of pointing up the relative absence of class conflict in the United States compared to the same period in France, when, from 1848 to 1851, a republican revolution "disintegrated in class war" (102). America in these years avoided internal conflict by "[e]scaping from the past into the West, from social crowds into nature, from class conflict into racial domination" (106). Thus Ahab in *Moby-Dick* (1851) "recontains shipboard class divisions" by "calling up primitive racial instincts"—the urge to dominate Indians and slaves in the imperial drive to mastery on which American freedom rests (129). For more recent works of literary and cultural studies that examine the complex politics of the American 1848, see Eric Lott, *Love and Theft*, and Shelley Streeby, *American Sensations*.

65. Quoted in Schlesinger, *Age of Jackson*, 451.

66. Preston King, quoted in Schlesinger, *Age of Jackson*, 451–52.

67. Quoted in Michael A. Morrison, *Slavery and the American West*, 109. See also Frederick J. Blue, *The Free Soilers*.

68. Philip S. Foner, *Business and Slavery*, 3.

69. Daniel L. Cohn, *Life and Times of King Cotton*, 85.

70. Quoted in Cohn, *Life and Times of King Cotton*, 80–81.

71. Sven Beckert, in *The Monied Metropolis*, describes the "cotton kingdom" as the primary "engine of profit" in the New York economy, allowing it to pull ahead of Philadelphia, Baltimore, and Boston. New York's traditional mercantile elite continued to dominate the city's economy through the antebellum period, making

up 40 percent of all taxpayers assessed in 1855 with assets exceeding ten thousand dollars (20). A small group of about 3,600 merchant families in 1855 owned approximately 28 percent of all real and personal wealth. Mercantile wealth was also concentrated at the top: in 1845 the richest 1 percent of families owned 47 percent of the city's noncorporate wealth, with the next 3 percent controlling a further 32 percent. See also E. Pessen, *Riches, Class, and Power*, 34, 48–49, 323–26.

72. John Ashworth, *Slavery, Capitalism, and Politics*, 444.

73. Quoted in Ashworth, *Slavery, Capitalism, and Politics*, 444.

74. Quoted in Eric Foner, *Free Soil, Free Labor, Free Men*, 91.

75. Charles Sumner, *Works*, 81.

76. See Rubin, *Historic Walt Whitman*, 179–80; Loving, *Walt Whitman*, 110–11.

77. Quoted in Rubin, *Historic Walt Whitman*, 223, 247.

78. Whitman, "Letters from a Travelling Bachelor," *New York Sunday Dispatch*, November 25, 1849, quoted in Rubin, *Historic Walt Whitman*, 338, 339.

79. Rubin, *Historic Walt Whitman*, 245.

80. Rollo G. Silver, "Whitman in 1850," 317. Erkkila argues that Whitman "conceived of the struggle against slavery as a class struggle against the feudal institutions of Europe" (*Whitman the Political Poet*, 46). While this is notably against the grain of a critical tradition that denies the existence of class struggle, Whitman's class animus was also directed closer to home.

81. John Russell Bartlett, *Dictionary of Americanisms*, 128. A torrent of political abuse was heaped on the Free-Soil Party created at Buffalo in August 1848 (with Whitman representing the Brooklyn Barnburners). Whigs and Democratic regulars denounced them as "whelps," "infidels," and "lousy curs," "zealots with turned coats," a "heterogeneous melange [*sic*] of incongruous anomalies." See Joseph G. Rayback, *Free Soil*, 245. "Words were neither minced nor mollified," one Free-Soiler recalled, "but made the vehicles of political wrath and the explosions of personal malice" (quoted in Rayback, 245). On Whitman's involvement with the Free-Soil Party, see Rubin, *Historic Walt Whitman*, 206–22.

82. See Eric Partridge, *A Dictionary of the Underworld*, 650–51.

83. Reynolds, *Walt Whitman's America*, 131. The parallel with James Russell Lowell's *Bigelow Papers* (1848) is instructive. Lowell, a Boston Brahmin and abolitionist, mixed the Yankee dialect of Hosea Bigelow with the orotund Latinity of the Reverend Homer Wilbur and combined these with "a swinging ballad metre, some sectional prejudice and vanity, some denunciation, some scriptural allusions, and

no cant" (quoted in Leon Howard, *Victorian Knight-Errant*, 234). As a "non-resistance" abolitionist, Lowell's politics were rather more radical than Whitman's, but the linguistic registers of *The Bigelow Papers* are kept clearly separated in the persons of the speakers. Hosea writes of how slavery "kind o' grates" his "narves," while the Rev. Wilbur chimes in with "It may be said of us all, *Exempla plus quam ratione vivimus*" ("We live more by example than reason") (50, 56). The effect produced is one of agreement across classes on the evils of slavery rather than dissension. In the patrician universe of Lowell's Boston, social hierarchies are maintained as the source of "humor," rather than aggressively breached, as they are in Whitman's satire.

84. John O'Sullivan, "White Slavery," 260.
85. O'Sullivan, "White Slavery," 261.
86. O'Sullivan, "White Slavery," 270.
87. O'Sullivan, "One of the Problems of the Age," 167.
88. O'Sullivan, "One of the Problems of the Age," 167.
89. O'Sullivan, "One of the Problems of the Age," 167.
90. Thomas R. Hietala, *Manifest Design*, 97.
91. O'Sullivan, "White Slavery," 261.
92. O'Sullivan, quoted in Anders Stephanson, *Manifest Destiny*, 42.
93. Stephanson, *Manifest Destiny*, 60.
94. Stephanson, *Manifest Destiny*, 59.
95. Arnold Guyot, *The Earth and Man*, 33.
96. Guyot, *The Earth and Man*, 33. On Guyot, see Henry Nash Smith, *Virgin Land*, 41–42. It was of course Smith who first described destinarian thinking in his critique of "the doctrine of the safety valve . . . an imaginative construction which masked poverty and industrial strife with the pleasing suggestion that a beneficent nature stronger than any human agency, the ancient resource of Americans, the power that had made the country rich and great, would solve the new problems of industrialism" (205–6).
97. The notebook is named after Jesse Talbot, the landscape artist, whose address at Wilson Street in Brooklyn was scribbled by Whitman inside the front cover. Talbot was "Whitman's frequent host and aesthetic tutor" in 1850 (Rubin, *Historic Walt Whitman*, 263). I have been guided by Grier's transcription in *NUPM*, vol. 1, checked against *TW*.
98. Whitman seems to have been particularly irked by genteel prescriptions against

beards, referring contemptuously in "Song of Myself" to the "scrape-lipped" and to "latherers" (*LG* 74, 81). The dress code of the Astor Opera House stipulated "freshly shaven faces," along with "evening dress, fresh waistcoats, and kid gloves" (quoted in Burrows and Wallace, *Gotham*, 762). The code enables Whitman to flourish a bristly beard as a badge of class defiance.

99. Efforts to establish the date of "Talbot Wilson" begin in 1921, with Emory Holloway's argument that the 1847 date occurring twice in the notebook in connection with Whitman's accounts means that his notes began in 1847, with the free verse lines of the latter part of the notebook made in 1849–50. In a 1953 article, Esther Sheppard argued for 1854, based on the similarity of "Talbot Wilson" to another notebook, "Poem Incarnating the Mind," which refers to the 1854 wreck of the *San Francisco*. It was Sheppard who first suggested that Whitman had written in the blank pages of an old notebook previously used for keeping his accounts. In 1968, Edward F. Grier examined a poor-quality microfilm of the notebook and decided that the two 1847 fiscal memoranda were the "strongest" evidence for "literary use around 1847" (quoted in Higgins, "Wage Slavery and the Composition of *Leaves of Grass*," 57). It was Grier who first conjectured "Mr. V. A." was Isaac Van Anden. In *NUPM*, vol. 1, Grier continued to argue that the account entries for 1847 must have held current interest for Whitman, since he kept them and excised others. A strong argument for a later date is made by Andrew C. Higgins, making use of the rediscovered notebook published on the Library of Congress website. Higgins decides that on page 83 (the "Mr. V. A. / 1847" page), "the interweaving of date and poetry is an illusion caused by the poor quality of the microfilm" (58). Able now to follow the actual pagination of the notebook, Higgins points out that page 83 is preceded by eight pages of stubs with account figures still visible—adding weight to Sheppard's contention that the fiscal memoranda are survivals from the notebook's earlier use and the notes and poetry of a later date. Higgins settles for a date of 1853–54, noting that, of the seven *Leaves of Grass* notebooks extant, four are positively dated 1854, leaving "an unexplained seven year silence" if the 1847 date is accepted (56). Higgins also argues that since these 1854 notebooks show a less mature style, it is unlikely that "Talbot Wilson" could have preceded them. Higgins uses the hypothesis of a later date to separate the notebook from the Free-Soil period, arguing that it was Whitman's "concern about class that propelled [him] towards poetry in the mid-1850s" rather than the issue of slavery (53). For Higgins, the notebook reveals a Whitman "far more concerned with issues of ownership and the soul," his discus-

sions "as much connected to working-class wage-slavery rhetoric as to Free Soil anti-chattel-slavery rhetoric" (61). I have been arguing that class conflict is an inseparable element of antislavery agitation in the period leading up to the 1850 poems; Higgins's belief that they must be somehow politically distinct is, I think, an oversimplification of a complex historical formation. For the purposes of my argument here, the important aspect of "Talbot Wilson" is that it *connects* the American 1848 with 1855—connects, that is to say, Whitman's Locofoco-Free-Soil past and his thinking about slavery and class with the thematic of life in class society that emerges in the clashing linguistic registers of *Leaves of Grass*. I am therefore persuaded by 1853–54 as a good date for "Talbot Wilson" but for rather different interpretive reasons than Higgins.

100. This is Stephanson's description of the New England abolitionist and minister, Theodore Parker. See Stephanson, *Manifest Destiny*, 54.

3. THE CLASS STRUGGLE IN LANGUAGE

1. Grier puts the date of this notebook as "obviously prior to 1855" and suggests it may antedate "Talbot Wilson," although some lines are not possible before January 1854 (*NUPM* 1:102).

2. According to Grier, these notes were "made before, or early in, 1855" (*NUPM* 1:169).

3. Other probable sources are J. D. Morrell's *Speculative Philosophy of Europe in the Nineteenth Century* (New York, 1849, 1853) and Joseph Gostwick's *German Literature* (Philadelphia, 1854). Carlyle's essay on Novalis is another likely source. See W. B. Fulglum, Jr., "Whitman's Debt to Joseph Gostwick," and Sister Mary Eleanor, "Hedge's *Prose Writers of Germany* as a Source of Whitman's Knowledge of German Philosophy."

4. Frederic H. Hedge, *Prose Writers of Germany*, 446.

5. Schelling, "On the Relation of the Plastic Arts to Nature," in *Prose Writers of Germany*, by Hedge, 510.

6. Hedge, *Prose Writers of Germany*, 509.

7. Schelling, "On the Relation of the Plastic Arts to Nature," in Hedge, 513. Italics mine.

8. Margaret A. Rose, *Parody: Ancient, Modern, and Post-Modern*, 8.

9. Rose, *Parody*. My thinking on these issues has been influenced by Rose's discussion in *Parody*, 47–50.

10. Fichte, "The Destination of Man," in *Prose Writers of Germany*, by Hedge, 385.

11. Fichte, "The Destination of Man," in Hedge, 385.

12. John Jump, *Burlesque* (1972), quoted in Rose, *Parody*, 57.

13. Lavater, "On the Nature of Man, Which Is the Foundation of the Science of Physiognomy," in *Prose Writers of Germany*, by Hedge, 191.

14. Lavater, "On the Nature of Man," in Hedge, 198.

15. Richard Chase identified "Song of Myself" as a poem "on the whole comic in tone," one taking "the specific form of American humor" (59). Chase brilliantly discussed the "sense of incongruous diversity" in the poem and noted that Whitman had "mastered at least the easier tricks of the native folk humor" (60, 73). But Chase did not identify Whitman's humor as satire or link his "shifts of ground between incongruous extremes" to class divisions in Whitman's society. Instead, following a critical tradition that sees Whitman's poetry as straightforwardly ameliorating in form and intention, Chase focused on Whitman's "transcendentalist" view of the colloquial as a way to "best unite the 'natural' and the 'spiritual'" (75, 91). Ronald Wallace, in *God Save the Clown*, notices the similarities between southwestern humor and the "robust and rhapsodic rowdiness" of Whitman's persona in "Song of Myself," but he does not analyze the style of southwestern humor in any detail or discuss Whitman's contributions to the genre in his New Orleans sketches. Wallace well describes humor in "Song of Myself" as "a force undercutting social prestige or pretense," and his arguments about how Whitman "deflates the experts by beating them at their own game" anticipate mine (56, 60). However, Wallace doesn't pursue an analysis of the class registers of language he detects in "Song," preferring instead to trace what he sees as the "archetypal comic patterns" of romance comedy in the poem.

16. Thomas Carlyle, *Sartor Resartus*, 22–23.

17. Carlyle, *Sartor Resartus*, 24.

18. Carlyle, quoted in G. B. Tennyson, *Sartor Called Resartus*, 241. The Whig critics perceived something lawless and insurrectionary about Carlyle's assault on Augustan evenness and decorum. Nathaniel L. Frothingham in the *Christian Examiner* noted how Carlyle "loves to bring together the low and the lofty, the learned and the vulgar, the strange and the familiar, the tragic and comic, into rather violent contrasts" (Jules Paul Seigel, 42). The *American Whig Review* found an analogy between Carlyle's subject matter, his prophecy of "the coming of democracy and of popular revolutions," and his style "utterly at variance with pure and classical forms."

Carlyle, a "literary monster and oddity," a "*vilaine* mangler of sentences," writes in
the style of revolution: he "selects fiery tints, and adopts cutting contrasts; his
lights are conflagrations of falling cities, his reflections from off the blood-pool of
massacre" ("Styles, American and Foreign," 352, 353). Henry David Thoreau
recalled the liberating effect Carlyle had on the younger generation of educated
New Englanders: Carlyle's style, "so diversified and variegated," captured "the
ceaseless tide of speech forever flowing in countless cellars, garrets, *parlors*," while
"emancipating the language" from "the fetters which a merely conservative, aim-
less, and pedantic literary class had imposed upon it," and setting an example of
"greater freedom and naturalness" (96, 93, 99). Emerson recorded in his journal
for 1835, "Charles [Emerson] says that to read Carlyle in N[orth] A[merican]
Review is like seeing your brother in jail" (*Journals*, vol. 5, 97). On the patrician
alarm over Carlyle, see John Paul Pritchard, *Literary Wise Men of Gotham*, 49–56.

19. Carlyle, "Jean Paul Friedrich Richter," 15.

20. See Joel C. Relihan, *Ancient Menippean Satire*, 12–26. On Menippean satire, see also
Mikhail Bakhtin, *Problems of Dostoevsky's Poetics*, 111–39. Eric Auerbach does not
treat the genre directly, but his discussion of "style-mingling" in Petronius,
Rabelais, and Montaigne is suggestive. See his *Mimesis: The Representation of Reality in Western Literature*, 24–49, 262–84, esp. 161–62.

21. Relihan, *Ancient Menippean Satire*, 26, 27.

22. Edwin S. Ramage, et al., *Roman Satirists*, 24; Relihan, *Ancient Menippean Satire*, 15.
See also Gay Sibley, "*Satura* from Quintilian to Joe Bob Briggs," 57–72.

23. R. Bracht Branham, *Unruly Eloquence*, 3.

24. Quoted in Christopher Robinson, *Lucian and His Influence in Europe*, 9.

25. Relihan, *Ancient Menippean Satire*, 44, 45.

26. Lucian, *Works of Lucian of Samosata*, 156, 157.

27. Lucian, *Works*, 130. Fred Manning Smith usefully discusses Carlyle's influence on
Whitman, but he doesn't consider the political meanings of Carlyle's style. See
"Whitman's Poet-Prophet and Carlyle's Hero" and "Whitman's Debt to Carlyle's
Sartor Resartus." The *Democratic Review* welcomed the publication by Putnam of
On Heroes, Hero-Worship, and the Heroic in History in an anonymous review that
recalled how "[a]t a period when elegance of diction and a sort of sickly senti-
mentality seemed to be the chief objects of literary attainment," Carlyle, by his
"boldness, depth, and originality of thought, and Scriptural simplicity of style,
infused a new and healthy vigor into the minds of men" (Review of *Heroes and*

Hero-Worship, 490). In the mid-1840s, Carlyle could thus be regarded as a sturdy Democrat, an ally of Young America in its struggle against the dominance of a fastidious mercantile elite.

28. Buell, *New England Literary Culture*, 343, 338. The incongruity was remarked by Charles Eliot Norton in his 1855 *Putnam's Monthly* review, although he also opines, rather sniffily, that Whitman's transcendentalism is old hat, as well as secondhand: "[a] fireman or omnibus driver, who had intelligence enough to absorb the speculations of that school of thought which culminated at Boston some fifteen or eighteen years ago, and resources of expression to put them forth again in a form of his own, with sufficient self-conceit and contempt for public taste to affront all usual propriety of diction," might, he says, have written "Song of Myself" (*CH* 25).

29. For the notion of culture as a particular kind of conversation between speakers who have unequal knowledge of foregoing conversations, see Kenneth Burke, *The Philosophy of Literary Form*, 110–11.

30. George Thompson, *Venus in Boston*, 1.

31. Thompson, *Venus in Boston*, 40.

32. David Reynolds observes that the novel features "society women" who "fantasize about having hundreds of lovers" but does not link Lady Hawley's speech and its imagery to this section of "Song of Myself" (*Beneath the American Renaissance*, 330). For a lively discussion of the political efficacy of Thompson's "urban pornogothic," see Christopher Looby, "George Thompson's 'Romance of the Real.'" Criticism of the restrictions of the domestic sphere was well established by the mid-1840s. Lydia Maria Child, in *Letters from New York*, lamented the "effects of a luxurious and artificial life" on young women, "continually checked by genteel limitations" and "left without ennobling objects of interest" (280, 281). In her *Lectures to Women on Anatomy and Physiology*, Mary S. Gove argued that, as a result of these "artificial and enervating habits," masturbation, or "the solitary vice," was "fearfully common" among women and "invade[d] all ranks" (244, 175, 177, 179). These public and private habits produce a distinctive bodily disposition. Gove includes a statement by "a lady of great worth and intelligence," who was "delicately reared, and took very little exercise," hence becoming "addicted to solitary vice" (180). "I had much dizziness, and my sight would often become entirely obscured, especially when I stooped and rose quickly," this lady notes (181). Gove later refers to "that stooping posture so common among young women who

destroy the contractility of the muscles by lacing" (189). Whitman, who reviewed Gove's book approvingly in the *Eagle* on September 26, 1846, had complained about "the atrocious custom" of "tight-lacing" as a strategy in the "warfare between nature and fashion" (*J2* 57, 58). In "Song of Myself," he pointedly juxtaposes the corseted, stooping body of the genteel female with a group of blacksmiths, the "lithe sheer of their waists" evoking the freely flowing productive labor of the artisanal male. On Gove and Whitman, see Reynolds, *Walt Whitman's America*, 202, 209.

33. Thompson, *Venus in Boston*, 65.
34. Thompson, *Venus in Boston*, 65.
35. Thompson, *Venus in Boston*, 14.
36. Thompson, *Venus in Boston*, 65.
37. Reynolds, *Beneath the American Renaissance*, 330.
38. Reynolds, *Beneath the American Renaissance*, 330, 331.
39. Thomas F. De Voe, *The Market Book* (1862), quoted in W. T. Lhamon, *Raising Cain*, 9.
40. Lhamon, *Raising Cain*, 2–3.
41. Leonore Lynne Fauley, *Black Dance in the United States*, 250.
42. Shane White and Graham White, *Stylin'*, 74.
43. Solomon Northup, *Twelve Years a Slave*, 217–18; also quoted in White and White, *Stylin'*, 84.
44. For the playbill, see Lhamon, *Raising Cain*, 26.
45. Lhamon, *Raising Cain*, 33.
46. W. A. Jones reached for the metaphor of artisanal labor as a corrective weight in an unbalanced literary order with an 1843 call, in the *Democratic Review*, for a poet with "mental energy answering to the strong right arm of the laborer," a poet whose words would "ring in every line like the short, quick blows on the anvil" ("Poetry for the People," 277).
47. Bercovitch, *Rites of Assent*, 46. The phrase "ritual of consensus" is Bercovitch's.
48. "Political Tolerance," 58.
49. "Political Tolerance," 64.
50. Bercovitch, *American Jeremiad*, 140.
51. "Political Tolerance," 64.
52. Alexander von Humboldt, *Cosmos*, 5. The phrase "nature's nation" comes from the title of the book by Perry Miller.

53. Blumin, "Explaining the New Metropolis," 18.

54. Hone, *Diary of Philip Hone*, 785.

55. Blumin, introduction to *New York by Gas-Light*, by Foster, 1.

56. Foster, *New York in Slices*, 7, 13.

57. Foster, *New York by Gas-Light*, 120.

58. Foster, *New York by Gas-Light*, 93.

59. Buckley, "Culture, Class, and Place in Antebellum New York," 34.

60. Cmiel, *Democratic Eloquence*, 53, 12–13.

61. Cmiel, *Democratic Eloquence*, 15.

62. Cmiel, *Democratic Eloquence*, 56, 57.

63. Cmiel, *Democratic Eloquence*, 58.

64. T. J. Clark, *Painting of Modern Life*, 259.

65. Michael P. Kramer observes that the passage reveals a "rudimentary" awareness of the main themes of mid-nineteenth-century philology: the "organic connection between national character and national language," the "putative differences between American English and British English," and the "growth of English and its resulting composite nature" (94). But Whitman's knowledge seems more than rudimentary here. James Perrin Warren dates Whitman's interest in language study from the second half of 1855, after the publication of *Leaves of Grass* and after his meeting with the philologist William Swinton ("Dating Whitman's Language Studies," 1–7). But, as Floyd Stovall notes, De Vere's book was reviewed briefly by Swinton in *Putnam's Monthly* for December 1853, and the review may well have attracted Whitman's attention (213). On Whitman's relation to debates on American English, see also Kenneth Cmiel, "'A Broad, Fluid Language of Democracy.'" For a reading of the ideological import of Whitman's linguistic theory and practice, see David Simpson, "Destiny Made Manifest: The Styles of Whitman's Poetry," 188–90. Simpson stresses the absorptive capacity of Whitman's language, whereas I argue for the continued class conflicts marked by its clashes of register.

66. Maximilian Schele De Vere, *Outlines of Comparative Philology*, 69, 81.

67. De Vere, *Outlines of Comparative Philology*, 118–19.

68. De Vere, *Outlines of Comparative Philology*, 120.

69. De Vere, *Outlines of Comparative Philology*, 187. Anglo-Saxonism is initially an elite preoccupation, part of a shift from "classical" to "romantic" values within literary culture that is traceable in the pages of the *North American Review*. The anonymous

reviewer of Erasmus Rask's *Grammar of the Anglo-Saxon Tongue* (1830) notes that "[t]he affectation of writing a Latinized or Frenchified tongue is, indeed, now quite discredited" and argues that words and idioms "of Anglo-Saxon growth" have "far more force and beauty" ("Anglo-Saxon Language and Literature," 325). Anglo-Saxonism can be seen as a reaction against the false refinements of the vulgar or the Latinate pretensions of the "middling." Longfellow satisfies this new elite taste with *Hyperion: A Romance*, welcomed by C. C. Felton for its "picturesque" use of the "old Saxon element" (148). The paradox is that an interest formerly confined to the elite has by midcentury become public property. In the course of noticing Louis F. Klipstein's *Analecta Anglo-Saxonica*, published by G. P. Putnam, an anonymous reviewer observes that enterprising publishers have given the "reading world" texts "till now to be found only in editions too rare and costly to be met within the private libraries of any but the wealthy" ("The Anglo-Saxon Race," 34). Such are the aesthetic vagaries—and the concealed politics—of the middle ground.

70. See John Swinton's "Rambles over the Realm of Verbs and Substantives," which echoes De Vere by stressing that English is "the most striking example of a composite language" and describing the process by which "an accession of Normanno-Franco-Celtic words was grafted on our ancient Saxon" (475, 476). Swinton associates Saxon with the "heart-life, pulsating with doings and darings" and Norman with "the outer and the conventional": Saxon demands "trouth, and freedom" while Norman is content with "honour" and "curtesie" (478). He also notes how Saxon donates the "affectionate terms father, mother, brother, sister," as well as "man" and "wife" (479). If Whitman had not read De Vere by early 1855, then it seems likely he had read Swinton's 1854 article.

71. Herder, "A Dialogue on Metempsychosis," in *Prose Writers of Germany*, by Hedge, 259. Emphasis mine.

72. Carlyle, *Sartor Resartus*, 50.

73. Herman Melville, *Moby-Dick; or, The Whale*, 257.

74. Rubin, *Historic Walt Whitman*, 161.

75. Wilentz, *Chants Democratic*, 258, 263.

76. Wilentz, *Chants Democratic*, 353.

77. Wilentz, *Chants Democratic*, 327, 329.

78. Thomas N. Baker, *Sentiment and Celebrity*, 100.

79. Baker, *Sentiment and Celebrity*, 104.

80. Quoted in Rubin, *Historic Walt Whitman*, 161.

81. *New York Herald*, May 9, 1849, quoted in "Muncipal Government," 487.

82. "Municipal Government," 483.

83. Evidence of General Hall to the Coroner's Court, quoted in "Municipal Government," 495.

84. "Municipal Government," 482.

85. H. M. Ranney, *Account of the Terrific and Fatal Riot*, 19. Ranney describes the Opera House on the night of May 10 as a microcosm of New York's stratified society: the private boxes "attended by the most wealthy and fashionable people"; the other, middle-class seats "let at a dollar admission"; the upper tier "reserved for people of humbler means or more modest pretensions, at seventy-five cents a ticket"; and, outside, the gathering mob "trying to force an entrance to the house, and throwing volleys of stones at the barricaded windows" (5). On the riot, see Paul A. Gilje, *Rioting in America*, 69–75; David Grimstead, *Melodrama Unveiled*, 68–74; Lawrence W. Levine, *Highbrow/Lowbrow*, 63–68.

86. Rubin, *Historic Walt Whitman*, 170.

87. Rubin, *Historic Walt Whitman*, 253–54.

88. Traubel, *With Walt Whitman in Camden*, 139. Stovall comments, "[h]is limited education and early practice of journalistic writing left him inadequately equipped to compete in polite letters. . . . If he had been a little more sophisticated he might have found congenial fellowship in the group gathered about E. A. Duyckinck . . . but his credentials, social perhaps as well as literary, were evidently unacceptable" (137). *To compete in polite letters*: Stovall's phrase serves as a reminder that the antebellum literary market in New York was occupied by gradations of the elite.

89. George N. Sanders, "Fogy Literature," 397.

90. See Bartlett, *Dictionary of Americanisms*. Blodgett and Bradley annotate "scarfed" as "[s]carified or channeled, hence lined or 'worn-down face'" (*RE* 74n). The *Dictionary of American English* has no such adjective, only the verb, to scarf, meaning "to cut off the body of a whale," and the noun, scarf, "a v-shaped or diagonal cut through a limb or tree." While Blodgett and Bradley's gloss is plausible, I think that scarf as an item of clothing fits the context of the pocket flaps better, evoking the smoothness of the ensemble disrupted by the intrusion of "grit."

91. Buell, *New England Literary Culture*, 158.

92. Buell, *New England Literary Culture*, 158.

93. Buell, *New England Literary Culture*, 160.

94. Reynolds, *Walt Whitman's America*, 325–26.

95. Rubin, *Historic Walt Whitman*, 270.

96. Rubin, *Historic Walt Whitman*, 305.

97. Rubin, *Historic Walt Whitman*, 305.

98. Charles Dickens, *American Notes*, 61, 62.

99. George Foster, *New York in Slices*, 22, 23, 24.

100. Solon Robinson, *Hot Corn*, 70–71.

101. Walter M. Gibson, *Prison of Weltevreden*, 120. The likelihood that Gibson is Whitman's source here is increased by a note dating from 1857 headed "Brutish human beings—Wild men—the 'Koboo:'" "Capt. Gibson affirms that all his statements in his book are true, and made in good faith. The 'koboo,' must be so" (*NUPM* 5:1976).

102. Gibson, *Prison of Weltevreden*, 181.

103. Guyot, *Earth and Man*, 33.

104. John North, *Fontana History of Astronomy and Cosmology*, 406.

105. Robert Chambers, *Vestiges of the Natural History of Creation*, 199.

106. Chambers, *Vestiges of the Natural History of Creation*, 9.

107. Chambers, *Vestiges of the Natural History of Creation*, 10. On Whitman's interest in astronomy, see Allen, *Solitary Singer*, 123–25.

108. Andrew Jackson Davis, *Principles of Nature*, 1. On Whitman and the Harmonists, a group of spiritualists who practiced "traveling clairvoyance" or "mental time-space travel," see Reynolds, *Walt Whitman's America*, 270–78, esp. 271.

109. Davis, *Principles of Nature*, 485.

110. Davis, *Principles of Nature*, 131.

111. Humboldt, *Cosmos: Sketches of a Physical Description of the Universe*, 5, 4.

112. Marx Edgeworth Lazarus, *Comparative Psychology and Universal Analogy*, viii.

113. Lazarus, *Comparative Psychology and Universal Analogy*, viii.

114. See Wilentz, *Chants Democratic*, 333.

115. Herder, "Dialogue on Metempsychosis," in *Prose Writers of Germany*, by Hedge, 255, 256.

116. Miller, *Nature's Nation*, 3.

117. Bercovitch, *American Jeremiad*, 157.

118. Bercovitch, *American Jeremiad*, 17, 26n.

119. Thomas Harman, *Caveat for Common Cursitors*, 114.

120. Robert Burns, *Poems and Songs*, 206, 207. Whitman later wrote approvingly of Burns as a writer "very close to the earth," describing his "Scotch patois" as "racy of the soil" (*PW* 2:560, 566). Whitman admired particularly Burns's "cantabile of jolly beggars in high jinks" (564). On the cant origins of "duds," see Partridge, *Dictionary of the Underworld*.

121. Nathaniel Hawthorne, "The New Adam and Eve," 248, 255. For Matthiessen, Whitman uses slang here with "no self-consciousness, but with the careless aplomb of a man speaking the language most natural to him" (526). But this begs the question of what is more "natural" in the line: the exhortation to "shoulder" one's "duds" or to "hasten forth"? Matthiessen elides the line's final clause, presumably because its stiff archaism doesn't match the loose-limbed spontaneity of its opening.

122. Carlyle, *On Heroes, Hero-Worship, and the Heroic in History*, 104–5.

POSTSCRIPT

1. Rourke, *American Humor*, 175.

2. Roy Harvey Pearce, *Historicism Once More*, 209–10, 212.

3. Jerome McGann, *Black Riders: The Visible Language of Modernism*, 114.

4. Roland Barthes, "Theory of the Text," 33.

5. Tzvetan Todorov, *Theories of the Symbol*, 174.

6. Michel Foucault, *The Order of Things*, 295.

7. Foucault, *Order of Things*, 303, 282.

8. Bergmann, *God in the Street*, 3.

9. Richard Terdiman, quoted in Bergmann, *God in the Street*, 20.

10. Wilson, *Figures of Speech*, 12.

11. Foucault, *Order of Things*, 295.

12. Foucault, *Order of Things*, 300.

13. Bakhtin, "Discourse in the Novel," 325. The etymology of "foofoo" is obscure. Bartlett notes the first occurrence in print as *A Glance at New York* and gives this definition: "[i]n New York, a slang word, meaning an 'outsider,' or one not in the secrets of a society, party or band" (158). In the 1877 edition, Bartlett modifies this to "a term of contempt, nearly equivalent to 'small potatoes,' a man not worth notice." The first edition of the *Oxford English Dictionary* describes "foo-foo," together with the variants "foofoo" and "fou-fou," as of West African origin, meaning "[a] kind of dough made out of plantains: a traditional food of Negroes

on both sides of the Atlantic." It cites Barclay's *Practical View of Slavery in the West Indies* (1826): "[a] negro . . . would greatly prefer his own good substantial dish of *foofoo*, composed of eddoes, ochras, and mashed plaintains." *OED* also notes that "foo" is an obsolete form of "foe." Perhaps black speech blended with white in the antebellum period in order to describe outsiders of all kinds, from plantains to small potatoes. For a discussion of the "increasing awareness" of New York City slang in the 1840s, see Stott, *Workers in the Metropolis*, 257–70, esp. 260.

14. Bakhtin, "Discourse in the Novel," 323–24.
15. Bakhtin, "Discourse in the Novel," 329.

BIBLIOGRAPHY

Aaron, Daniel. *Writers on the Left: Episodes in American Literary Communism*. New York: Columbia UP, 1992.

Abrahams, Edward. *The Lyrical Left: Randolph Bourne, Alfred Stieglitz, and the Origins of Cultural Radicalism in America*. Charlottesville: UP of Virginia, 1987.

Adkins, Nelson F. "James K. Paulding's *Lion of the West*." *American Literature* 3.3 (1931): 249–58.

Agnew, Jean-Christophe. *Worlds Apart: The Market and the Theater in Anglo-American Thought, 1550–1750*. Cambridge: Cambridge UP, 1986.

Allen, Gay Wilson. *The New Walt Whitman Handbook*. New York: New York UP, 1975.

——. *The Solitary Singer: A Critical Biography of Walt Whitman*. New York: Macmillan, 1955.

"Anglo-Saxon Language and Literature." *North American Review* 33.73 (1831): 325–51.

"The Anglo-Saxon Race." *North American Review* 73.152 (1851): 34–71.

Arac, Jonathan. "F. O. Matthiessen: Authorizing an American Renaissance." *The American Renaissance Reconsidered*. Ed. Walter Benn Michaels and Donald E. Pease. Baltimore: Johns Hopkins UP, 1989. 90–112.

——. "Whitman and Problems of the Vernacular." *Breaking Bounds: Whitman and American Cultural Studies*. Ed. Betsy Erkkila and Jay Grossman. New York: Oxford UP, 1996. 44–61.

Arpad, Joseph J. Introduction. *A Narrative of the Life of David Crockett of the State of Tennessee, Written by Himself*. By David Crockett. New Haven: College and UP, 1972. 7–38.

Arvin, Newton. *Whitman*. New York: Russell, 1969.

Ashworth, John. *Slavery, Capitalism, and Politics in the Antebellum Republic*. Vol. 1, *Commerce and Compromise, 1820–1850*. Cambridge: Cambridge UP, 1995.

Aspiz, Harold. "Walt Whitman: The Spermatic Imagination." *American Literature* 56 (1984): 379–95.

Asselineau, Roger. *The Evolution of Walt Whitman: The Creation of a Personality*. Cambridge: Harvard UP, 1960.

Auerbach, Eric. *Mimesis: The Representation of Reality in Western Literature*. Trans. Willard R. Trask. Princeton: Princeton UP, 1953.

Augst, Thomas. "Antebellum Authorship and the Common Property of American Literature." *Reviews in American History* 32.3 (2004): 358–64.

———. *The Clerk's Tale: Young Men and Moral Life in Nineteenth-Century America*. Chicago: U of Chicago P, 2003.

Baker, Benjamin A. *A Glance at New York*. 1848. *On Stage America! A Selection of Distinctly American Plays*. Ed. Walter J. Meserve. New York: Prospero, 1996.

Baker, Thomas N. *Sentiment and Celebrity: Nathaniel Parker Willis and the Trials of Literary Fame*. New York: Oxford UP, 1999.

Bakhtin, Mikhail. "Discourse in the Novel." *The Dialogic Imagination: Four Essays*. Trans. Caryl Emerson and Michael Holquist. Austin: U of Texas P, 1990. 259–422.

———. *Problems of Dostoevsky's Poetics*. Trans. Caryl Emerson. Manchester: Manchester UP, 1984.

Bank, Rosemarie K. *Theatre Culture in America, 1825–1860*. Cambridge: Cambridge UP, 1997.

Barker-Benfield, G. J. "The Spermatic Economy: A Nineteenth-Century View of Sexuality." *The American Family in Social-Historical Perspective*. Ed. Michael Gordon. New York: St. Martin's, 1978. 374–402.

Baron, Dennis E. *Grammar and Good Taste: Reforming the American Language*. New Haven: Yale UP, 1982.

Barthes, Roland. "Theory of the Text." 1973. *Untying the Text: A Post-Structuralist Reader*. Ed. Robert Young. London: Routledge, 1990. 31–47.

Bartlett, John Russell. *Dictionary of Americanisms: A Glossary of Words and Phrases Usually Regarded as Peculiar to the United States*. 2nd ed. Boston: Little, 1859.

"Bartlett's *Dictionary of Americanisms*." *North American Review* 69.144 (1849): 94–110.

Beach, Christopher. *The Politics of Distinction: Whitman and the Discourses of Nineteenth-Century America*. Athens: U of Georgia P, 1996.

Beckert, Sven. *The Monied Metropolis: New York City and the Consolidation of the American Bourgeoisie, 1850–1896*. Cambridge: Cambridge UP, 2001.

Bercovitch, Sacvan. *The American Jeremiad*. Madison: U of Wisconsin P, 1978.

———. *The Rites of Assent: Transformations in the Symbolic Construction of America*. New York: Routledge, 1993.

Bergmann, Hans. *God in the Street: New York Writing from the Penny Press to Melville*. Philadelphia: Temple UP, 1995.

Blair, Hugh. *Lectures on Rhetoric and Belles Lettres*. Vol. 1. London: Richardson, 1823.

Blair, Walter. *Native American Humor*. New York: Chandler, 1960.

Blake, Casey Nelson. *Beloved Community: The Cultural Criticism of Randolph Bourne, Van Wyck Brooks, Waldo Frank, and Lewis Mumford*. Chapel Hill: U of North Carolina P, 1990.

Blue, Frederick J. *The Free Soilers: Third Party Politics, 1848–54*. Urbana: U of Illinois P, 1973.

Blumin, Stuart M. *The Emergence of the Middle Class: Social Experience in the American City, 1760–1900*. Cambridge: Cambridge UP, 1989.

———. "Explaining the New Metropolis: Perception, Depiction, and Analysis in Mid-Nineteenth-Century New York City." *Journal of Urban History* 11.1 (1984): 9–38.

Boucicault, Dion. *The Poor of New York*. 1857. *American Melodrama*. Ed. Daniel C. Gerould. New York: Performing Arts Journal Publications, 1992.

Bowers, Fredson. *Whitman's Manuscripts: Leaves of Grass (1860); A Parallel Text*. Chicago: U of Chicago P, 1955.

Branham, R. Bracht. *Unruly Eloquence: Lucian and the Comedy of Traditions*. Cambridge: Harvard UP, 1989.

Brewer, E. Cobham. *The Dictionary of Phrase and Fable*. 1894. New York: Avenel, 1978.

Bryant, William Cullen. *Poetical Works*. Vol. 1. Ed. Parke Godwin. New York: Russell, 1967.

Buckley, Peter G. "Culture, Class, and Place in Antebellum New York." *Power, Culture, and Place: Essays on New York City*. Ed. John Hull Mollenkopf. New York: Sage Foundation, 1988. 25–52.

Buell, Lawrence. *New England Literary Culture: From Revolution through Renaissance*. Cambridge: Cambridge UP, 1989.

Burke, Kenneth. *The Philosophy of Literary Form*. Baton Rouge: Louisiana State UP, 1941.

Burns, Robert. *The Poems and Songs of Robert Burns*. Vol. 1, *Text*. Ed. James Kinsley. Oxford: Clarendon, 1968.

Burrows, Edwin G., and Mike Wallace. *Gotham: A History of New York City to 1898*. New York: Oxford UP, 1999.

Byrdsall, F. *The History of the Loco-Foco, or Equal Rights Party, Its Movements, Conventions and Proceedings; with Short Characteristic Sketches of Its Prominent Men*. 1842. New York: Burt Franklin, 1967.

Callan, Norman. "Augustan Reflective Poetry." *The Pelican Guide to English Literature*. Vol. 4, *From Dryden to Johnson*. Ed. Boris Ford. Harmondsworth, Eng.: Penguin, 1968. 346–71.

Carlyle, Thomas. "Jean Paul Friedrich Richter." *Critical and Miscellaneous Essays*. Vol. 1. London: Chapman, 1893. 1–25.

———. *On Heroes, Hero-Worship, and the Heroic in History*. 3rd ed. London: Chapman, 1846.

———. *Sartor Resartus*. Oxford: Oxford UP, 1987.

Cawelti, John G. *Apostles of the Self-Made Man*. Chicago: U of Chicago P, 1965.

Cayton, Mary Kupiec. "The Making of an American Prophet: Emerson, His Audiences, and the Rise of the Culture Industry in Nineteenth-Century America." *American Historical Review* 92.3 (1987): 597–620.

Chambers, Robert. *Vestiges of the Natural History of Creation*. New York: Harper, 1857.

Channing, William E. "Self-Culture." *A Selection from the Works of William E. Channing, D.D.* Boston: American Unitarian Association, 1855. 399–464.

Charvat, William. *The Origins of American Critical Thought, 1810–1835*. New York: Russell, 1968.

Chase, Richard. *Walt Whitman Reconsidered*. London: Gollancz, 1955.

Child, Lydia Maria. *Letters from New York. Second Series*. New York: Francis, 1845.

Clark, T. J. *The Painting of Modern Life: Paris in the Art of Manet and His Followers*. London: Thames, 1985.

Cmiel, Kenneth. "'A Broad, Fluid Language of Democracy': Discovering the American Idiom," *Journal of American History* 79.3 (1992): 913–36.

———. *Democratic Eloquence: The Fight over Popular Speech in Nineteenth-Century America*. New York: Morrow, 1990.

Cohn, Daniel L. *The Life and Times of King Cotton*. New York: Oxford UP, 1956.

Cox, James M. "Humor of the Old Southwest." *The Comic Imagination in American Literature*. Ed. Louis D. Rubin. New Brunswick: Rutgers UP, 1973. 101–12.

Davis, Andrew Jackson. *The Principles of Nature, Her Divine Revelations, and a Voice to Mankind*. New York: Lyon, 1852.

De Certeau, Michel. *The Practice of Everyday Life*. Trans. Steven Rendall. Berkeley: U of California P, 1988.

De Vere, Maximilian Schele. *Outlines of Comparative Philology*. New York: Putnam, 1853.

Dickens, Charles. *American Notes for General Circulation*. London: Chapman, 1850.

Diggins, John Patrick. *The Rise and Fall of the American Left*. New York: Norton, 1992.

Ditz, Toby. "Shipwrecked; or, Masculinity Imperiled: Mercantile Representations of Failure and the Gendered Self in Eighteenth-Century Philadelphia." *Journal of American History* 81.1 (1994): 51–80.

Dorson, Richard M. "Mose the Far-Famed and World-Renowned." *American Literature* 15 (September 1943): 288–300.

Eleanor, Mary. "Hedge's *Prose Writers of Germany* as a Source of Whitman's Knowledge of German Philosophy." *Modern Language Notes* 61 (1946): 381–88.

Emerson, Ralph Waldo. "English Literature: Introductory." *Early Lectures of Ralph Waldo Emerson*. Vol. 1, *1833–1836*. Ed. Stephen E. Wincher and Robert Spiller. Cambridge: Harvard UP, 1966. 217–32.

———. *Journals and Miscellaneous Notebooks*. Ed. William H. Gilman, et al. 11 vols. Cambridge: Harvard UP, 1960–1975.

———. *Poems*. Boston: Houghton, 1895.

———. "The Poet." *The Early Lectures of Ralph Waldo Emerson*. Vol. 3, *1838–1842*. Ed. Robert E. Spiller and Wallace E. Williams. Cambridge: Harvard UP, 1972. 347–65.

———. "The Present State of Ethical Philosophy." *Two Unpublished Essays*. Ed. Edward Everett Hale. Boston: Lamson, 1896. 43–81.

———. "Spiritual Laws." *The Collected Works of Ralph Waldo Emerson*. Vol. 2, *Essays: First Series*. Ed. Joseph Slater. Cambridge: Harvard UP, 1979. 75–96.

"The English Language." *Knickerbocker* 15 (March 1840): 212–20.

Erkkila, Betsy. "Walt Whitman: The Politics of Language." *American Studies* 24.2 (1983): 21–34.

———. *Whitman the Political Poet*. New York: Oxford UP, 1989.

Fauley, Leonore Lynne. *Black Dance in the United States, from 1619 to 1970*. Diss. U of Southern California, 1971.

Felton, C. C. "Hyperion." *North American Review* 50.106 (January 1840): 145–61.

Fichtelberg, Joseph. *Critical Fictions: Sentiment and the American Market, 1780–1870*. Athens: U of Georgia P, 2003.

Fiedler, Leslie. "Images of Walt Whitman." *"Leaves of Grass" One Hundred Years After*. Ed. Milton Hindus. Stanford: Stanford UP; London: Oxford UP, 1955. 55–73.

Folsom, Ed. *Walt Whitman's Native Representations*. Cambridge: Cambridge UP, 1997.

Foner, Eric. *Free Soil, Free Labor, Free Men: The Ideology of the Republican Party before the Civil War*. New York: Oxford UP, 1970.

Foner, Philip S. *Business and Slavery: The New York Merchants and the Irrepressible Conflict*. Chapel Hill: U of North Carolina P, 1941.

Foster, George G. *New York by Gas-Light and Other Urban Sketches*. 1850. Ed. Stuart M. Blumin. Berkeley: U of California P, 1990.

———. *New York in Slices: By an Experienced Carver*. New York: Burgess, 1849.

Foucault, Michel. *The Order of Things: An Archaeology of the Human Sciences*. London: Tavistock, 1974.

Fowler, O. S. *Amativeness; Or, Evils and Remedies of Excessive and Perverted Sexuality: Including Warning and Advice to the Married and Single, Being a Supplement to "Love and Parentage."* 13th ed. New York: Fowlers, 1848.

Fulglum, W. B., Jr. "Whitman's Debt to Joseph Gostwick." *American Literature* 12 (1941): 491–97.

Fussell, Edwin. *Lucifer in Harness: American Meter, Metaphor, and Diction*. Princeton: Princeton UP, 1973.

Gibson, Walter M. *The Prison of Weltevreden; and a Glance at the East Indian Archipelago*. New York: Riker, 1855.

Gilje, Paul A. *Rioting in America*. Bloomington: Indiana UP, 1996.

Gorman, Bryan K. "'Heroic Spiritual Grandfather': Whitman, Sexuality, and the American Left, 1890–1940." *American Quarterly* 52.1 (2000): 90–126.

Gorn, Elliott J. "'Good-Bye Boys, I Die a True American': Homicide, Nativism, and Working Class Culture in Antebellum New York City." *Journal of American History* 74.2 (1987): 388–410.

Gove, Mary S. *Lectures to Women on Anatomy and Physiology*. New York: Harper, 1846.

Gramsci, Antonio. *Selections from the Prison Notebooks of Antonio Gramsci*. Trans. Quintin Hoare and Geoffrey Nowell-Smith. London: Lawrence, 1971.

Greenspan, Ezra. "Some Remarks on the Poetics of 'Participle-Loving Whitman.'" *The Cambridge Companion to Walt Whitman*. Ed. Ezra Greenspan. Cambridge: Cambridge UP, 1995. 92–109.

Grimstead, David. *Melodrama Unveiled: American Theater and Culture, 1800–1850*. Berkeley: U of California P, 1968.

Gronowicz, Anthony. *Race and Class Politics in New York City before the Civil War*. Boston: Northeastern UP, 1998.

Grossman, Allen. "The Poetics of Union in Whitman and Lincoln: An Inquiry toward the Relationship of Art and Poetry." *The American Renaissance*

Reconsidered. Ed. Walter Benn Michaels and Donald E. Pease. Baltimore: Johns
Hopkins UP, 1989. 183–208.

Gutman, Herbert G. *Work, Culture, and Society in Industrializing America: Essays in
American Working-Class Social History*. New York: Knopf, 1976.

Guyot, Arnold. *The Earth and Man: Lectures on Comparative Physical Geography in Its
Relation to the History of Mankind*. 1849. Trans. C. C. Felton. Boston: Gould, 1860.

Habermas, Jurgen. *Legitimation Crisis*. Trans. Thomas McCarthy. London:
Heinemann, 1976.

Harlow, Alvin F. *Old Bowery Days: The Chronicles of a Famous Street*. New York:
Appleton, 1931.

Harman, Thomas. *A Caveat for Common Cursitors*. 1566. *The Elizabethan Underworld: A
Collection of Tudor and Early Stuart Tracts and Ballads Telling of the Lives and
Misdoings of Vagabonds, Thieves, Rogues and Cozeners, and Giving Some Account of
the Operation of the Criminal Law*. Ed. A. V. Judges. London: Routledge, 1930.
61–118.

Haswell, Charles H. *Reminiscences of an Octogenarian of the City of New York (1816 to
1860)*. New York: Harper, 1896.

Hawthorne, Nathaniel. "The New Adam and Eve." *The Centenary Edition of the Works
of Nathaniel Hawthorne*. Vol. 10, *Mosses from an Old Manse*. Ed. J. Donald Crowley.
Columbus: Ohio State UP, 1974.

Hedge, Frederic H. *Prose Writers of Germany*. Philadelphia: Carey, 1848.

Hietala, Thomas R. *Manifest Design: Anxious Aggrandizement in Late Jacksonian
America*. Ithaca: Cornell UP, 1985.

Higgins, Andrew C. "Wage Slavery and the Composition of *Leaves of Grass*: The
'Talbot Wilson' Notebook." *Walt Whitman Quarterly Review* 20 (2002): 53–77.

Hirschkop, Ken. *Mikhail Bakhtin: An Aesthetic for Democracy*. Oxford: Oxford UP,
1999.

Hirschkop, Ken, and David Shepperd. "Bakhtin and the Politics of Criticism."
PMLA 109.1 (1994): 116–18.

Hofstadter, Richard. *The American Political Tradition*. London: Cape, 1967.

Hone, Philip. *The Diary of Philip Hone, 1828–1851*. Ed. Allan Nevins. New York: Dodd,
1969.

Horlick, Allan S. *Country Boys and Merchant Princes: The Social Control of Young Men in
New York*. Lewisburg, PA: Bucknell UP, 1975.

Howard, Leon. *Victorian Knight-Errant: A Study of the Early Literary Career of James Russell Lowell*. Westport, CT: Greenwood, 1971.

Humboldt, Alexander von. *Cosmos: Sketches of a Physical Description of the Universe*. Vol. 1. Trans. Edward Sabine. 3rd ed. London: Longman, 1847.

Hyde, Lewis. *The Gift: Imagination and the Erotic Life of Property*. New York: Random, 1983.

Jones, W. A. "Criticism in America." *United States Democratic Review* 15.75 (1844): 241–49.

———. "Poetry for the People." *Democratic Review* 13.63 (1843): 266–79.

Kerber, Linda K. *Federalists in Dissent: Imagery and Ideology in Jeffersonian America*. Ithaca: Cornell UP, 1970.

Killingsworth, M. Jimmie. *Whitman's Poetry of the Body: Sexuality, Politics, and the Text*. Chapel Hill: U of North Carolina P, 1989.

Kramer, Michael P. *Imagining Language in America: From the Revolution to the Civil War*. Princeton: Princeton UP, 1992.

Lasch, Christopher. *The True and Only Heaven: Progress and Its Critics*. New York: Norton, 1991.

Laurie, Bruce. *Artisans into Workers: Labor in Nineteenth-Century America*. New York: Hill, 1989.

———. *Working People of Philadelphia, 1800–1850*. Philadelphia: Temple UP, 1980.

LaValley, Albert J. *Carlyle and the Idea of the Modern: Studies in Carlyle's Prophetic Literature and Its Relation to Blake, Nietzsche, Marx, and Others*. New Haven: Yale UP, 1968.

Lazarus, Marx Edgeworth. *Comparative Psychology and Universal Analogy*. Vol. 1, *Vegetable Portraits of Character, Compiled from Various Sources, with Original Additions*. New York: Fowlers, 1851.

Lears, Jackson. *Fables of Abundance: A Cultural History of Advertising in America*. New York: Basic, 1994.

———. "Reconsidering Abundance: A Plea for Ambiguity." *Getting and Spending: European and American Consumer Societies in the Twentieth Century*. Ed. Susan Strasser, Charles McGovern, and Matthias Judt. Cambridge: Cambridge UP, 1998. 449–66.

Leggett, William. *A Collection of the Political Writings of William Leggett*. Ed. Theodore Sedgwick. 2 vols. New York: Taylor, 1840.

Lehuu, Isabelle. *Carnival on the Page: Popular Print Media in Antebellum America*. Chapel Hill: U of North Carolina P, 2000.

Levine, Lawrence W. *Highbrow/Lowbrow: The Emergence of Cultural Hierarchy in America*. Cambridge: Harvard UP, 1990.

Lewis, R. W. B. *The American Adam: Innocence, Tragedy, and Tradition in the Nineteenth Century*. Chicago: U of Chicago P, 1955.

Lhamon, W. T., Jr. *Raising Cain: Blackface Performance from Jim Crow to Hip Hop*. Cambridge: Harvard UP, 1998.

Liebman, Sheldon W. "The Development of Emerson's Theory of Rhetoric, 1821–1836." *American Literature* 41 (1969): 178–206.

Livingston, James. "Modern Subjectivity and Consumer Culture." *Getting and Spending: European and American Consumer Societies in the Twentieth Century*. Ed. Susan Strasser, Charles McGovern, and Matthias Judt. Cambridge: Cambridge UP, 1998. 413–29.

———. *Pragmatism and the Political Economy of Cultural Revolution, 1850–1940*. Chapel Hill: U of North Carolina P, 1994.

Looby, Christopher. "George Thompson's 'Romance of the Real': Transgression and Taboo in American Sensation Fiction." *American Literature* 65.4 (December 1993): 651–72.

Lott, Eric. *Love and Theft: Blackface Minstrelsy and the American Working Class*. New York: Oxford UP, 1993.

Loving, Jerome. *Walt Whitman: The Song of Himself*. Berkeley: U of California P, 1999.

Lowell, James Russell. *The Bigelow Papers (First Series): A Critical Edition*. Ed. Thomas Wortham. Dekalb: Northern Illinois UP, 1977.

———. "Emerson the Lecturer." *The Writings of James Russell Lowell*. Vol. 1, *Literary Essays*. London: Macmillan, 1890. 349–60.

Lucian. *Works of Lucian of Samosata*. Vol. 1. Trans. H. W. Fowler and F. G. Fowler. London: Oxford UP, 1939.

Lunettes, Henry [Margaret Cockburn Conkling]. *The American Gentleman's Guide to Politeness and Fashion*. New York: Derby, 1858.

MacKay, Charles. *Life and Liberty in America; or, Sketches of a Tour in the United States and Canada in 1857–1858*. New York: Harper, 1859.

Macpherson, C. B. *The Political Theory of Possessive Individualism: Hobbes to Locke*. Oxford: Oxford UP, 1964.

Marx, Karl. *Capital*. Vol. 1. Trans. Ben Fowkes. Harmondsworth, Eng.: Penguin, 1976.

———. *Early Writings*. Trans. Rodney Livingstone and Gregor Benton. Harmondsworth, Eng.: Penguin, 1975.

———. *Grundrisse: Foundation of the Critique of Political Economy (Rough Draft)*. Trans. Martin Nicolaus. Harmondsworth, Eng.: Penguin, 1973.

Maslan, Mark. *Whitman Possessed: Poetry, Sexuality, and Popular Authority*. Baltimore: Johns Hopkins UP, 2001.

Mason, Jeffrey B. *Melodrama and the Myth of America*. Bloomington: Indiana UP, 1993.

Mathews, Cornelius. "The Late Ben. Smith, Loafer." *Knickerbocker Magazine* 6.1 (1835): 63–67.

———. *Man in the Republic: A Series of Poems*. 2nd ed. New York: Paine, 1846.

———. *A Pen-and-Ink Panorama of New York City*. New York: Taylor, 1853.

"Mathews's Poems." *North American Review* 58.123 (1844): 509–11.

Matthiessen, F. O. *American Renaissance: Art and Expression in the Age of Emerson and Whitman*. London: Oxford UP, 1941.

Mayer, Arno J. "The Lower Middle Class as Historical Problem." *Journal of Modern History* 47 (1975): 409–36.

McGann, Jerome. *Black Riders: The Visible Language of Modernism*. Princeton: Princeton UP, 1993.

McGill, Meredith L. *American Literature and the Culture of Reprinting, 1834–1853*. Philadelphia: U of Pennsylvania P, 2003.

McWilliams, John P., Jr. *The American Epic: Transforming a Genre, 1770–1860*. Cambridge: Cambridge UP, 1989.

Melville, Herman. *Moby-Dick; or, The Whale*. Harmondsworth, Eng.: Penguin, 1972.

Mencken, H. L. *The American Language: An Inquiry into the Development of English in the United States*. 4th ed. New York: Knopf, 1957.

Meyers, Marvin. *The Jacksonian Persuasion: Politics and Belief*. Stanford: Stanford UP, 1960.

Miller, E. H. *Walt Whitman's Poetry: A Psychological Journey*. New York: New York UP, 1968.

Miller, Perry. *Nature's Nation*. Cambridge: Harvard UP, 1967.

———. *The Raven and the Whale: The War of Words and Wits in the Era of Poe and Melville*. New York: Harcourt, 1956.

Mirsky, D. "Poet of American Democracy." *Walt Whitman: A Critical Anthology.* Ed. Francis Murphy. Harmondsworth, Eng.: Penguin, 1969. 238–55.

Moon, Michael. *Disseminating Whitman: Revision and Corporeality in "Leaves of Grass."* Cambridge: Harvard UP, 1991.

Morrison, Michael A. *Slavery and the American West: The Eclipse of Manifest Destiny and the Coming of the Civil War.* Chapel Hill: U of North Carolina P, 1997.

Morson, Gary Saul. Introduction to the Russian cluster. *PMLA* 107.2 (1992): 226–31.

Mulcaire, Terry. "Publishing Intimacy in *Leaves of Grass.*" *ELH* 60 (1993): 471–501.

"Municipal Government." *Democratic Review* 25.132 (June 1849): 481–500.

"New Publications." *Brooklyn Daily Times* December 17, 1856. Walt Whitman Archive. http://www.iath.virginia.edu/whitman/ar...leaves/leaves56/

Newfield, Christopher. "Democracy and Male Homoeroticism." *Yale Journal of Criticism* 6.2 (1993): 29–62.

North, John. *The Fontana History of Astronomy and Cosmology.* London: Fontana, 1994.

Northup, Solomon. *Twelve Years a Slave: Narrative of Solomon Northup, a Citizen of New-York, Kidnapped in Washington City in 1841, and Rescued in 1853, from a Cotton Plantation near the Red River, in Louisiana.* Auburn, NY: Derby, 1853.

O'Sullivan, John. "One of the Problems of the Age." *Democratic Review* 14.68 (1844): 156–67.

———. "White Slavery." *Democratic Review* 11.51 (1842): 260–72.

Parker, Hershel. *Herman Melville: A Biography.* Vol. 1, *1819–1851.* Baltimore: Johns Hopkins UP, 1996.

Partridge, Eric. *A Dictionary of the Underworld: British and American.* London: Routledge, 1961.

———. *Slang: Today and Yesterday.* 4th ed. London: Routledge, 1970.

Pascal, Richard. "'Dimes on the Eyes': Walt Whitman and the Pursuit of Wealth in America." *Nineteenth-Century Literature* 42.2 (1989): 142–72.

Paulding, James Kirke. *The Lion of the West, Retitled The Kentuckian, or A Trip to New York.* Revised by John Augustus Stone and William Bayle Bernard. Ed. James N. Tidwell. Stanford: Stanford UP, 1954.

Pearce, Roy Harvey. *Historicism Once More: Problems and Occasions for the American Scholar.* Princeton: Princeton UP, 1969.

Pease, Donald. "Walt Whitman's Revisionary Democracy." *The Columbia History of American Poetry.* Ed. Jay Parini. New York: Columbia UP, 1993. 148–71.

Perry, Bliss. *Walt Whitman: His Life and Work*. London: Constable; Boston: Houghton, 1906.

Pessen, E. *Riches, Class, and Power before the Civil War*. Lexington, MA: Heath, 1973.

"The Philosophy of the Ancient Hindus." *Massachusetts Quarterly Review* 4 (September 1848): 401–22.

Pickering, John. *A Vocabulary, or Collection of Words and Phrases Which Have Been Supposed to Be Peculiar to the United States of America*. Boston: Cummings, 1816.

"Political Tolerance." *Democratic Review* 3.9 (1838): 58–65.

Porte, Joel. "Transcendental Antics." *Veins of Humor*. Ed. Harry Levin. Cambridge: Harvard UP, 1972. 167–84.

"The Portico, Number Five." *Knickerbocker* 9 (1837): 47–51.

Pritchard, John Paul. *Literary Wise Men of Gotham: Criticism in New York, 1815–1860*. Baton Rouge: Louisiana State UP, 1963.

Ramage, Edwin S., David L. Sigsbee, and Sigmund C. Fredericks. *Roman Satirists and Their Satire: The Fine Art of Criticism in Ancient Rome*. Park Ridge, NJ: Noyes, 1974.

Ranney, H. M. *Account of the Terrific and Fatal Riot at the New York Astor Place Opera House*. New York: Ranney, 1849.

Rayback, Joseph G. *Free Soil: The Election of 1848*. Lexington: UP of Kentucky, 1970.

Relihan, Joel C. *Ancient Menippean Satire*. Baltimore: Johns Hopkins UP, 1993.

Review of *Leaves of Grass*, by Walt Whitman. *New York Daily News* February 27, 1856. *Walt Whitman Archive*. http://www.virginia.edu/whitman/works/leaves/1855/reviews (January 7, 2003).

Review of *Leaves of Grass*, by Walt Whitman. *Washington Daily National Intelligencer* February 18, 1856. *Walt Whitman Archive*. http://www.iath.virginia.edu/whitman/works/leaves/1855/reviews (October 17, 2000).

Review of *On Heroes, Hero-Worship, and the Heroic in History*, by Thomas Carlyle. *Democratic Review* 19.102 (1846): 490.

Reynolds, David S. *Beneath the American Renaissance: The Subversive Imagination in the Age of Emerson and Melville*. Cambridge: Harvard UP, 1989.

———. *Walt Whitman's America: A Cultural Biography*. New York: Knopf, 1995.

Robinson, Christopher. *Lucian and His Influence in Europe*. London: Duckworth, 1979.

Robinson, Solon. *Hot Corn: Life Scenes in New York Illustrated*. New York: De Witt, 1854.

Rogin, Michael Paul. *Fathers and Children: Andrew Jackson and the Subjugation of the American Indian*. New York: Knopf, 1975.

———. *Subversive Genealogy: The Politics and Art of Herman Melville*. Berkeley: U of California P, 1985.

Rorabaugh, W. J. *The Craft Apprentice: From Franklin to the Machine Age in America*. New York: Oxford UP, 1986.

Rose, Margaret A. *Parody: Ancient, Modern, and Post-Modern*. Cambridge: Cambridge UP, 1993.

Rourke, Constance. *American Humor: A Study of the National Character*. New York: Harcourt, 1931.

Rubin, Joseph Jay. *The Historic Walt Whitman*. University Park: Pennsylvania State UP, 1973.

Sanders, George N. "Fogy Literature: A Short Chapter." *Democratic Review* 30.167 (1852): 396–400.

Scarry, Elaine. *The Body in Pain: The Making and Unmaking of the World*. New York: Oxford UP, 1985.

Schlesinger, Arthur M., Jr. *The Age of Jackson*. London: Eyre, 1946.

Scott, Donald M. "The Popular Lecture and the Creation of a Public in Mid-Nineteenth-Century America." *Journal of American History* 66.4 (1980): 791–809.

Seigel, Jules Paul, ed. *Thomas Carlyle: The Critical Heritage*. London: Routledge, 1971.

Sellers, Charles. *The Market Revolution: Jacksonian America, 1815–1846*. New York: Oxford UP, 1991.

Shklar, Judith N. *American Citizenship: The Quest for Inclusion*. Cambridge: Harvard UP, 1991.

Sibley, Gay. "*Satura* from Quintilian to Joe Bob Briggs: A New Look at an Old Word." *Theorizing Satire: Essays in Literary Criticism*. Ed. Brian A. Connery and Kirk Combe. New York: St. Martin's, 1995. 57–72.

Silver, Rollo G. "Whitman in 1850: Three Uncollected Articles." *American Literature* 19 (1948): 301–17.

Simpson, David. "Destiny Made Manifest: The Styles of Whitman's Poetry." *Nation and Narration*. Ed. Homi Bhabha. London: Routledge, 1990. 177–96.

Simpson, Lewis P. "Federalism and the Crisis of Literary Order." *American Literature* 32.3 (1960): 253–66.

Smith, Fred Manning. "Whitman's Debt to Carlyle's *Sartor Resartus*." *Modern Language Quarterly* 3 (1942): 51–65.

———. "Whitman's Poet-Prophet and Carlyle's Hero." *PMLA* 55.4 (1940): 1146–64.

Smith, Henry Nash. *Virgin Land: The American West as Symbol and Myth*. Rev. ed. Cambridge: Harvard UP, 1970.

Smith-Rosenberg, Caroll. *Disorderly Conduct: Visions of Gender in Victorian America*. New York: Oxford UP, 1985.

Sommer, Doris. "Supplying Demand: Walt Whitman as the Liberal Self." *Reinventing the Americas: Comparative Studies of the Literature of the United States and Spanish America*. Ed. Bell Gale Chevigny and Gari Laguardia. Cambridge: Cambridge UP, 1986.

Stansell, Christine. *City of Women: Sex and Class in New York, 1789–1860*. New York: Knopf, 1986.

Stephanson, Anders. *Manifest Destiny: American Expansionism and the Empire of Right*. New York: Hill, 1995.

Stokes, Melvyn, and Stephen Conway, eds. *The Market Revolution in America: Social, Political, and Religious Expressions, 1800–1880*. Charlottesville: UP of Virginia, 1996.

Stott, Richard B. *Workers in the Metropolis: Class, Ethnicity, and Youth in Antebellum New York City*. Ithaca: Cornell UP, 1990.

Stovall, Floyd. *The Foreground of "Leaves of Grass."* Charlottesville: UP of Virginia, 1974.

Streeby, Shelley. *American Sensations: Class, Empire, and the Production of Popular Culture*. Berkeley: U of California P, 2002.

Strong, George Templeton. *The Diary of George Templeton Strong*. Vol. 1. Ed. Allan Nevins and Milton Halsey Thomas. New York: Macmillan, 1952.

"Styles, American and Foreign: Carlyle and His Imitators." *American Whig Review* 15.88 (1852): 349–56.

"Success in Life." *Harper's New Monthly Magazine* 7.38 (July 1853): 238–40.

Sumner, Charles. *The Works of Charles Sumner*. Vol. 2. Boston: Lee, 1870–1883.

Swinton, John. "Rambles over the Realm of Verbs and Substantives." *Putnam's Monthly Magazine* 4.23 (1854): 472–81.

Tennyson, G. B. *Sartor Called Resartus: The Genesis, Structure, and Style of Thomas Carlyle's First Major Work*. Princeton: Princeton UP, 1965.

Thomas, M. Wynn. *The Lunar Light of Whitman's Poetry*. Cambridge: Harvard UP, 1987.

———. "Whitman and the Dreams of Labor." *Walt Whitman: The Centennial Essays*. Ed. Ed Folsom. Iowa City: U of Iowa P, 1994. 133–52.

————. "Whitman's Tale of Two Cities." *American Literary History* 6.4 (1994): 633–57.

Thompson, E. P. "The Moral Economy of the English Crowd in the Eighteenth Century." *Customs in Common*. Harmondsworth, Eng.: Penguin, 1993. 185–258.

Thompson, George. *Venus in Boston: A Romance of City Life*. New York: Berry, 1849.

Thoreau, Henry David. "Thomas Carlyle and His Works." *The Writings of Henry David Thoreau*. Vol. 10, *Miscellanies*. Boston: Houghton, 1893. 81–130.

Thornton, R. H. *An American Glossary: Being an Attempt to Illustrate Certain Americanisms upon Historical Principles*. London: Francis, 1912.

Tocqueville, Alexis de. *Democracy in America*. Vol. 2. Trans. Henry Reeve. Ed. Phillips Bradley. New York: Vintage, 1990.

Todorov, Tzvetvan. *Theories of the Symbol*. Trans. Catherine Porter. Oxford: Blackwell, 1982.

Traubel, Horace. *With Walt Whitman in Camden*. Vol. 1. New York: Rowman, 1961.

Turner, Victor S. *Dramas, Fields, and Metaphors: Symbolic Action in Human Society*. Ithaca: Cornell UP, 1974.

————. *From Ritual to Theatre: The Human Seriousness of Play*. New York: PAJ, 1982.

————. *The Ritual Process: Structure and Anti-Structure*. Chicago: Aldine, 1969.

Wallace, Ronald. *God Be with the Clown: Humor in American Poetry*. Columbia: U of Missouri P, 1984.

Warner, Michael. "Whitman Drunk." *Breaking Bounds: Whitman and American Cultural Studies*. Ed. Betsy Erkkila and Jay Grossman. New York: Oxford UP, 1996. 30–43.

Warren, James Perrin. "Dating Whitman's Language Studies." *Walt Whitman Quarterly Review* 1 (1983): 1–7.

————. *Walt Whitman's Language Experiment*. University Park: Pennsylvania State UP, 1990.

Webster, Noah. *An American Dictionary of the English Language*. Rev. ed. Springfield, MA: Merriam, 1859.

White, Shane, and Graham White. *Stylin': African American Expressive Culture from Its Beginnings to the Zoot Suit*. Ithaca: Cornell UP, 1998.

Whitman, Walt. *An American Primer: With Facsimiles of the Original Manuscript*. Ed. Horace Traubel. London: Putnam, 1904.

————. *Collected Writings of Walt Whitman, The Journalism*. Ed. Herbert Bergman. 2 vols. New York: Lang, 1998–2003.

————. "Death of the Veteran Brooklyn Printer." *Brooklyn Daily Eagle* December 31,

1859. Rpt. In "A Tribute to William Hartshorne: Unrecorded Whitman."
William White. *American Literature* 42 (1971): 554–58.

———. *The Early Poems and the Fiction*. Ed. Thomas L. Brasher. New York: New York UP, 1963.

———. *The Gathering of the Forces*. Ed. Cleveland Rogers and John Black. 2 vols. New York: Putnam, 1920.

———. *Leaves of Grass: Reader's Edition*. Ed. Harold W. Blodgett and Scully Bradley. London: U of London P, 1965.

———. *New York Dissected: A Sheaf of Recently Discovered Newspaper Articles by the Author of "Leaves of Grass."* Ed. Emory Holloway and Ralph Adimari. New York: Wilson, 1936.

———. *Notebooks and Unpublished Prose Manuscripts*. Ed. Edward F. Grier. 6 vols. New York: New York UP, 1984.

———. *Prose Works 1892*. Ed. Floyd Stovall. 2 vols. New York: New York UP, 1964.

———. "Talbot Wilson" notebook. American Memory. Library of Congress. http://www.memory.loc.gov/ammem/wwhtml/wwcoll.html.

———. *Uncollected Poetry and Prose of Walt Whitman*. Ed. Emory Holloway. 2 vols. London: Heinemann, 1922.

———. *Walt Whitman: The Critical Heritage*. Ed. Milton Hindus. London: Routledge, 1971.

———. *Walt Whitman's Leaves of Grass: The First (1855) Edition*. Ed. Malcolm Cowley. New York: Penguin, 1986.

———. *Walt Whitman's Workshop*. Ed. Clifton Furness. New York: Russell, 1964.

Widmer, Edward. *Young America: The Flowering of Democracy in New York City*. New York: Oxford UP, 2000.

Wilentz, Sean. *Chants Democratic: New York City and the Rise of the American Working Class, 1788–1850*. New York: Oxford UP, 1986.

Wilson, R. Jackson. *Figures of Speech: American Writers and the Literary Marketplace, from Benjamin Franklin to Emily Dickinson*. New York: Knopf, 1989.

Zboray, Ronald J. *A Fictive People: Antebellum Economic Development and the American Reading Public*. New York: Oxford UP, 1993.

Zweig, Paul. *Walt Whitman: The Making of the Poet*. New York: Basic, 1984.

INDEX

Kean, Charles, 79

Knickerbocker Magazine, 35, 37–38, 73, 82

Knickerbocker elite, 35, 37–38, 79

laissez-faire, 17, 19, 71; Whitman and, 88

Latinate diction, 29, 36, 38, 42, 47, 69, 72, 74, 75, 76, 78, 87, 120n36, 131–32n69; in Lowell, *Bigelow Papers*, 123–24n83

Lavater, Johann Kaspar, 61

Lazarus, Marx Edgeworth, 94

Lears, Jackson, 26, 27

Leaves of Grass preface, 15–16, 24, 33, 74–75

Leggett, William, 15, 16, 17, 53

Liebig, Justus, 30

Livingston, James, 26

Locofoco faction, 14–15, 113–14n51; Whitman's Locofoco sentiments, 53, 55, 58, 69, 84, 94, 98, 126n99

Longstreet, Augustus Baldwin, 41

Lowell, James Russell, 123–24n83

lower middle class, 8; and autodidacticism in Whitman, 34, 46, 104; and cultural aspiration, 65, 80–82; and market society, 2; and need for hygiene, 17, 87, 90; artisans as, 7; as ambiguous class location, 80, 82, 111–12n33; as insecure class location, 82, 85, 91; as linguistic and cultural "middle ground," 72, 76; autodidacticism characteristic of, 90; clerks as, 7, 27–28; *Franklin Evans* as story of, 10; journalists as, 9; laissez-faire as tenet of, 17; Matthiessen's critique of Whitman as, 32; shift of

values within, 23; Tocqueville on, 8; Whitman's identification with, 11–12, 26–27; Whitman's family as, 8–9

Lucian, 63–64

Macpherson, C. B., 12

Macready, Charles, 80

"The Madman," 9

Manifest Destiny, 49–50, 71; Whitman and, 15, 50–51, 54–55, 96

market economy, 3, 7, 12, 17–18, 21, 28, 88. *See also* laissez-faire

market revolution, 12, 26

market society, 2, 5, 13, 18

Marx, Karl, 13, 14, 21, 23

masturbation, 17–20; and spermatic economy, 18–19, 115–16n69; and upper-class women, 66–67; Gove on, 129–30n32

Mathews, Cornelius, 79; "The Late Ben Smith, Loafer," 30; *Man in the Republic*, 39; *A Pen-and-Ink Panorama of New York City*, 7, 9

Matthiessen, F. O., 1, 32

McGann, Jerome, 101

Melville, Gansevoort, 38

Melville, Herman, 78, 122n64

Mencken, H. L., 40

Menippean satire, 63–64. *See also* seriocomic style

merchant elite, 35, 39, 42, 65, 72, 73, 79, 81. *See also* aristocracy, *Knickerbocker Magazine*, neoclassicism, slavocracy, upper class, Upper Ten Thousand

Mexican War, 44, 50–51

THE IOWA WHITMAN SERIES

Conserving Walt Whitman's Fame:
  Selections from Horace Traubel's Conservator, *1890–1919,*
  edited by Gary Schmidgall

Intimate with Walt:
  Selections from Whitman's Conversations with Horace Traubel,
  1888–1892, edited by Gary Schmidgall

The Pragmatic Whitman:
  Reimagining American Democracy, by Stephen John Mack

Transatlantic Connections:
  Whitman U.S., Whitman U.K., by M. Wynn Thomas

Visiting Walt:
  Poems Inspired by the Life and Work of Walt Whitman,
  edited by Sheila Coghill and Thom Tammaro

Walt Whitman and the Class Struggle,
  by Andrew Lawson

Walt Whitman and the Earth:
  A Study in Ecopoetics, by M. Jimmie Killingsworth

Walt Whitman:
  The Correspondence, Volume VII, edited by Ted Genoways

Whitman East and West:
  New Contexts for Reading Walt Whitman, edited by Ed Folsom